PEREGRINATION 22

Philip Purser

SAPERE
BOOKS

PEREGRINATION
22

Published by Sapere Books.

24 Trafalgar Road, Ilkley, LS29 8HH

saperebooks.com

ISBN: 978-0-85495-547-3

CHAPTER ONE

On the last of the month Telegems Productions (Marylebone) Ltd went quietly out of business with a formal notice in the *London Gazette* and a sly paragraph in the *Evening Standard* diary, and I was out of a job again. I bore Gibbings no particular ill will. It wasn't altogether his fault. We went over to the Gluepot for a Guinness apiece.

'What I'll do,' said Gibbings, 'is fire you as from last week. Then I can pay you off with three months' salary.'

'Thanks a million.'

'Now look, old boy. I'm only trying to help. You were on a two-year contract. It has eight months to go. You can take your chance with the other creditors if you like. But you may get only two bob or half-a-crown in the pound.'

'Okay,' I said. 'Thanks.'

'If only we could have sold the Simon de Montfort series in America we'd have been laughing,' said Gibbings wistfully.

'I told you we needed an American as Simon.'

'I know, I know. We tried to get Jeff Chandler. He was too expensive. Anyway, Bobby did jolly well. Everyone said so, especially in the jousts and things. I didn't know he had it in him.'

I made a non-committal noise.

We drank up. 'Give me a ring in a couple of months' time,' said Gibbings. 'Maybe I'll have things straightened out a bit by then.'

'Fine,' I said. 'Sorry about everything.'

On the bus I thought, 'Wouldn't it be nice — just once — to work for a big solid firm, a firm that lasted.' Somehow I had always been with furtive little ones that didn't. There had been *Whither?*, the magazine of travel and adventure, published from two rooms and a sink in Victoria. It lasted sixteen months. There had been Hessian Films, who made two second features and went bust as a third was about to go on the floor, script by me. There had been Harman and Levis, publishers (as it turned out) to the remainder trade. Two years, that one.

The flat was empty and tidy. It was one of Mrs Johnson's days and she had cleared up fiercely. She was a great one for the clearing up. The trouble was it didn't seem to leave her time for any actual cleaning. I found a packet of frozen rice in the fridge and a packet of frozen prawns, and thought maybe I would make a curry thing. But the saucepan wasn't clean. To be exact it was coated with some mangled remains of spaghetti from the night before. Mrs Johnson, the wily old cow, had put it aside pretending she thought I might want them.

There was also a bottle of Cyprus white wine, strong and resinous. I poured a glass, took it into the living-room and sat down at the desk and began to sort out accumulated papers. I always did this when a job finished. It was a sort of ritual taking stock. This one yielded the usual bills, a couple of receipts, an invitation to a christening, and an insurance proposal I'd never done anything about. I shovelled them back into a drawer and my hand encountered a little pear-shaped bottle.

Odorono. Jane had left it behind that morning six months ago. I drove her to the airport and we hovered like dead souls in the departure lounge until the Tannoy said its piece. 'Please take leave of your friends.'

That was the phrase. I'd always meant to use it for a title. The last I saw of her was disappearing into the grubby aluminium side of the Constellation. She wrote once; that was all.

I suppose we'd been so happy together because neither of us expected it to last and neither of us wanted it to. Not at the time, anyway. It was a nice affair, a convenient affair, a no-one-gets-hurt summery sunny affair, even when the moment came to go home to New Zealand (Invercargill, actually) and marry that meat merchant. Jane had always said that it would be easier never to question her going, but accept it as inevitable and indisputable, something outside speculation. Only as I drove home alone from the airport did I question the decision. Only three days later, on the first Saturday afternoon after her going, did I cry for her.

Now for the first time it occurred to me that it had been rather tough on the meat merchant. Still, what the eye doesn't see … I decided I'd better eat. The prawns, still locked together in an icy cube, seemed hardly enough. I walked up the street to the Idée Fixe which, at the time, was cheap and quite good. The *Telegraph* discovered it while I was in the Arctic and now it's hell.

They gave me a table at the back, between the Ladies' and the cupboard where they used to keep all the salt cellars and pepper mills. I was surveying the place to see if there wasn't something better when I saw Peregrine Potter dining in solitude in the opposite corner. I suppose this must be rated one of those Chance Meetings from which spring the whole story. I always used to be a bit sceptical about them when I was reading Buchan and people at about twelve or thirteen. In fairness, though, I should add that I did run into Peregrine quite often. Two or three times a year, anyway. It wasn't a very long Chance.

His real name was Stanley Potter, but by sheer persistence over the years he had accustomed everyone to calling him Peregrine. He saw me about the same time as I saw him and waved a fork. I went over and joined him.

'How are things?' he said. 'Nice to see you.'

'Not so hot, as a matter of fact. The television thing folded up. Today, actually.'

Peregrine's round face registered sympathy. He was small and neat and sandy. 'That's tough,' he said. 'Very tough.' The little wheels were turning already. Presently he would ask me what I was going to do now.

Peregrine and I had been together on *Whither?* In fact, we had been the whole staff. Undeterred by the failure of Whitherism in print Peregrine had gone on to put it into practice. He started a little travel agency specializing in the off-beat.

He sent liberal couples from Highgate bicycling through Andalusia, economists tramping round Limousin and lady school-teachers exploring a Danish island with nonconformist traditions and houses thatched in seaweed. Oddly enough it prospered.

'What will you do now?' said Peregrine.

'Dunno, really. Freelance I should think. I've got some ideas for television plays. Land a film if I'm lucky.'

'Mm,' said Peregrine, mouth full of escalope maison. I knew what he was leading up to. More than once, between jobs, I'd been glad of a spot of seasonal employment in the travel business. I'd been six weeks behind the counter one time, and couriered two parties to a Berlin Festival another.

'How about helping me out again?' he said finally.

I simulated a little surprise. 'Well, thanks very much. I'd like to.' At least it paid the rent. 'But I don't want to get too involved. You know, something might turn up unexpectedly.'

'That's all right. You can come strictly on an *ad hoc* basis.' Peregrine had been in the B.B.C. during the war.

CHAPTER TWO

I started the following week, walking along to Peregrine's three basement offices behind Victoria Street about ten in the morning and catching a 39 bus back in the evening about six thirty. Peregrine never said anything about hours to me; I tried to keep fairly regular ones out of consideration for the rest of the staff, which comprised a lady called Mrs Windern and a secretary, Dim Doreen. It was early in the season and the tempo was still relaxed.

A regular client called Dancer, a shy bachelor of private means, who for some reason was always referred to as 'friend Dancer', began his annual vacillation over where to go, and six music lovers from Sidcup got lost in Aachen. We rescued them by phone. Then on the Wednesday Peregrine brought me a dusty file that was vaguely familiar.

'I wonder if you'd take on the Peregrination 22 business,' he said apologetically.

Had we been characters in a B-picture (International mystery set in Polar terrain, exciting after slow start but leave the kids at home; scenery tops) there should have been a chord here from the main menace theme. As it was, all that happened was that I registered some bleak surprise.

'God, is that still going on?'

'I'm afraid so,' said Peregrine. 'And more of a muddle than ever. But something may yet come out of it.'

The holiday brochure which Peregrine sent out every year was called *Peregrinations*, neatly enough; and every holiday it contained was identified by the word Peregrination followed by a number. Peregrination 13 was the walking tour through

Limousin, Peregrination 15 the Speleological Fortnight in the Pyrenees.

Peregrination 22 had been set up in proof every year since anyone could remember, and every year it had been dropped again before *Peregrinations* went to Press. You jumped from Peregrination 21 (Ten Days with the Nomadic Lapps) to 23 (In the Footsteps of the Commandos — Narvik and the Lofotens). Peregrination 22 was called Fifteen Days of Adventure in the Arctic, and was an old idea of Peregrine's. It had figured in the pages of *Whither?* before he had started the agency. It was set in Spitsbergen and if it could be fixed up it would be the offest off-beat holiday in anybody's brochure.

Spitsbergen is five hundred miles north of Norway and only six hundred short of the North Pole. Mainly snow and ice, with some coal mines. In winter it is dark twenty-four hours a day and in summer it is broad daylight twenty-four hours a day. It is the most northerly inhabited area in the world. Peregrine, who had once been there for a couple of days, reckoned it could be also the most exciting.

'What's been happening that's new?' I asked.

'Was a German called Randers involved last time you were here?'

'Don't think so. But I know Randers, don't I?'

'Of course. You met him at the Berlin Festival. He's my correspondent there now. Started a little agency rather like mine.'

At the time of the Festival he'd been a sort of official interpreter cum public relations man. We had some mildly riotous times together.

I said, 'He had a girlfriend in England he was always on about. Miss Somebody-or-other. They went to theatres together, but always to *Call Me Madam*. They'd seen it four times.'

'Really?' said Peregrine impatiently. 'Anyway, that's the main development. He wants to do what I've always wanted to do, so we've more or less joined forces. At least I hope we have. He seems rather to have gone astray lately.'

We carted the file back into Peregrine's inner sanctum, and went through it. All along, the trouble with the Spitsbergen business had been the absence of anywhere to stay in the place. There was a nice little steamer service from Tromsø on which we occasionally sent people. But they had to stay aboard the whole trip. There were no hotels ashore.

'Randers suggested we should set up our own hotel,' said Peregrine. 'Well, not exactly a hotel — a kind of little guesthouse we could have there and open up each summer.'

'Good idea!' I said. 'Where would it be?'

'That's the trouble. I'm not sure any more. It was going to be Ny Alesund. That's the more northerly Norwegian settlement, you know. They were coming round to the idea of letting us have one of the old timber houses there to do up. It was all but settled. Then Randers went and got a different idea. This was the letter.'

I took it. It was in English, the curiously foreign English which even fluent English-speakers produce when they try to write it.

'You see,' said Peregrine, 'he wants to go somewhere else now. Up in a fjord called Krossfjorden. That's further north again and absolutely in the wilds. Not a soul for miles. It's madness.'

'There's some abandoned mine there, he's been told,' I said, reading the letter. 'And two or four buildings which would be obliging. Do you think he looked up the wrong word?'

'I suppose so. Anyway, he's run into trouble. The land in question belongs to a British firm.' He passed me another letter. 'He can't locate it and wants our help. He's supposed to be coming over here again soon, so will you see what you can hunt up?'

I took the file home and systematically brought myself up to date on a long story. The letters at the back I half remembered from previous spells with Peregrine. Mostly they were from the Norwegian government or the shipping companies which served Spitsbergen — or Svalbard, as it is properly known. Strictly speaking the name Spitsbergen refers only to the main island of the archipelago.

Yes, said the first letter, dated 1952 or thereabouts, tourists would be most welcome. There was a steamer service which made the round trip from Tromsø in Northern Norway in eleven days, calling at Longyear City, Ny Alesund, and several other places of interest: as there were no hotels in Svalbard, however, passengers would not be allowed to stay ashore between calls.

Some routine correspondence followed concerning clients of Peregrine who had made the trip. Then a reiteration from Oslo that tourists could not stay ashore, except in the case of scientific expeditions fully accredited by the Norwegian Polar Institute. Leaflets from the shipping companies. Grudging permission for an ornithologist to stay in Ny Alesund if he could arrange accommodation with the mining company. A cordial letter from the Governor of Svalbard inviting Mr Potter, personally, to stay at his official residence any time he should visit the islands.

I moved on to more recent developments. There was a fresh approach from Peregrine about the possibilities of renting accommodation, and a reply from Norway that for the first time was mildly encouraging. It mentioned the name of Randers as someone who was similarly interested. Then came a letter from Randers himself: he had been told Mr Potter was ambitious towards Svalbard; perhaps they could combine exertions.

The exertions in question fared tolerably well. A letter from the coal company in Ny Alesund expressed the belief that a timber hostel building might be made available on a temporary basis between late June and early September. Work in the mines was much reduced after a serious accident underground. Any conversion of the building would have to be approved in advance.

Randers chimed in with an alternative proposal: across the fjord from Ny Alesund was New London, an abandoned marble-mining site with some old buildings still standing, though doubtless much fallen-in. Why should they not start a permanent house there? It was only a kilometre or two by motor-boat across the fjord. Peregrine's reply was non-committal but not very enthusiastic.

Finally came Randers's latest proposal, that they should leave Ny Alesund altogether and go into the next fjord north, Krossfjorden. There, he said, was another abandoned mine whose buildings were said to be most upright. There was also suitable ground for an encampment, whatever he meant by that. The land belonged to a company called the Caledonian Spitsbergen Development Corporation. He, Randers, could find no record of it. Could we help? He would be coming to London in May.

In the next few days I made what inquiries I could, but Whitsun was approaching and business in Peregrine's three rooms mounted daily. Dim Doreen, the secretary, was sent along to Bush House with a shilling in her little hot hand, but as we might have guessed, the Caledonian Spitsbergen Development Corporation was a Scottish company registered in Edinburgh. A contact of Peregrine's in the travel business there dug up the name of a firm of solicitors, Ferguson, Roberts and Holburn, S.S.C. I wrote and had an acknowledgment but nothing more. Then I got involved in a protracted wrangle over the allocation of nine available couchettes among eleven teachers and forty-three pupils of varying sex who intended to go by train to Pisa on August Bank Holiday Saturday.

Also, friend Dancer cancelled his Peregrination 36 (Sun Worshipper's Seminar on the Ile du Levant) and applied tentatively for 27 (Through the Land of the Sagas on Pony back). Peregrination 22 had rather to be set aside until Randers could come.

Away from the office my agent said he was reasonably hopeful of getting me a writing assignment on a picture to be called *Vice Girl*, and in the square where I lived the blossom was out on the trees.

CHAPTER THREE

'In Germany we are also having such traffic,' said Randers.

'But it is not allowed to stop in this manner.'

'It's not quite so bad as this always,' I said irritably. 'There's a State Visit or something. This is the season for them. Many roads are closed.' As ever when talking to Germans I found myself putting everything into simple declarative sentences.

We were in a taxi in the middle of a solid wedge of hooting, overheated transport between Birdcage Walk and Victoria. A policeman in Gilbert and Sullivan ceremonial uniform surveyed the scene tolerantly.

'I shall not catch the train,' sighed Randers. 'Miss Penywern will have anxiety.' Miss Penywern — that was the name of the girlfriend. She lived at Reigate.

'Never mind. There'll be another twenty minutes later.'

'That is so,' said Randers. 'Well, we must not waste this time wholly.' He rummaged in a briefcase for his papers. 'It is agreed, then, that you will make an expedition to Edinburgh?'

'Yes, I'll do that. But you mustn't think that will commit us in any way. Mr Potter is still much keener on the original idea of a guesthouse at Ny Alesund.'

'Ah, the new sheem is much better. Such a beautiful setting. The air so pure. The scenery so breath-taking. We will have the — the Brighton of the Arctic!' Randers had made a funny remark. His mouth curved at the corners in a sudden comical grin.

He had one of those faces that are half matinée idol and half clown: in repose, rather handsome in a worldly way, with a lined brow and hair receding in a deep 'M'; as soon as he laughed becoming much more of an amiable mug. You noticed then how his nose turned up and his chin drifted away. He was thirty-eight-ish and could be irritating after a long spell, but I liked him well enough for short periods.

I said, 'This new place — Krossfjorden. Where did you hear about it?'

Randers hesitated. 'Someone has told me, who has been there. Mr Potter been to Svalbard at all?'

'Just for one or two days, I think. On a North Sea cruise. He used to be quite a traveller. Now he's married and got children he goes to Broadstairs every year.'

'Ah, yes.'

The taxi had crawled within sight of the Victoria Palace. The posters caught Randers's eye.

'So many theatres,' he exclaimed. 'I am jealous of all your theatres.'

'Berlin is not so badly off,' I said primly. 'When I was there for the festival I saw Brecht and Buechner and *Waiting for Godot* long before they were heard of here.'

'Yes, yes,' said Randers vaguely. 'We have nice theatres too. But have you seen *Salad Days*?'

'No, actually I haven't.'

'Oh, you must. It is so beautiful. Miss Penywern and I have seen it twice. We have nothing like *Salad Days* in Germany.' He started to sing, in an unexpected falsetto:

'Summer and sunshine
And falling in love…'

I walked up to the ticket barrier with him. There was a train in ten minutes. Randers was deep in thought.

'If Mr Potter is going — where did you say?'

'Broadstairs.'

'Ah, yes, if Mr Potter is going to Broadstair then perhaps he will not be coming to Svalbard?'

'I didn't know he was planning to go.'

'Really? But it was all settled. I am going in Julie — how is it? Ju-*ly*? In July. Just the there-and-back voyage on the steamer but it will be enough to see all the places. Some — er — colleagues will be there. And Mr Potter, I have thought.'

As a matter of fact Peregrine had muttered something about making a trip to Spitsbergen again, but as he'd toyed with this idea every year I'd known him I hadn't attached much importance to it. Anyway, it was unthinkable that he would leave the agency in mid-season.

I said, 'I should think it's unlikely.'

Randers said triumphantly, 'Then you must come in his place, Colin! We will have big fun!'

'Not possible, I'm afraid.'

'But why not, Col? I mean it. I am serious. Someone must be coming from England, I think. It shall be you.'

'Well, we'll see,' I said comfortably. At the moment nothing was further from my thoughts than any trip to the snow and ice. My world was all around, the world of the big red buses moored outside the station. 'Give my regards to Miss Penywern.'

'Oh thank you,' said Randers. 'I shall.'

All the same, I raised the matter with Peregrine when I got back to the office. He wrinkled his nose and said yes, he had been hoping to make the trip. But now the work was piling up as usual. 'Why are people so helpless when it comes to enjoying themselves?' he asked plaintively.

'I dunno, but it's your bread-and-butter.'

'The more you organize them the happier they seem,' Peregrine admitted. 'Anyway, about this Spitsbergen thing: would *you* like to go?'

'Good God, I shouldn't think so. I've never thought about it. It doesn't sound quite me, really. I mean, haven't you got any business in St Tropez that needs looking into?'

'No, seriously. I think you might like this one. A chance to go somewhere really interesting. Expenses paid — well, most of them.' (Peregrine was always cautious.) 'All I'd want, apart from some sense on this hotel-wretched-guesthouse business, would be your reactions to the trip as a trip. Whether you found the place exciting. What the weather's like or does it get too cold? What the steamer's like. The food, accommodation. How the whole itinerary hangs together.'

Peregrine cocked his head to one side in professional expectation. I pondered. I didn't really want to be away from London while jobs were in the air.

'Could I think about it?'

'Of course.'

CHAPTER FOUR

I flew up to Edinburgh the next day but one, on the morning plane. The trip would hardly have been worthwhile solely for the Spitsbergen inquiry: Peregrine also wanted something lined up with a Scottish shipping company who were organizing cruises to the Faeroes. I disposed of that first, had some lunch, and walked up the Mound to the Scottish companies register, which is in Parliament House along with the law offices and Court of Session. I hunted through the index, paid my bob search fee, and was presently handed the massive file on the Caledonian Spitsbergen Development Corporation.

The pages were old and musty-brown. The company had been formed in 1925 to make mineralogical surveys in West Spitsbergen. Three years later it had been expanded to start active mining operations on a site of 102 square miles leased under the terms of the Svalbard Treaty of 1920. In 1930 it had acquired a further tract of land, fifty-eight square miles. The share capital of the expanded company was £10,000 in £1 shares.

I flipped forward to later days. Clearly the company had been inactive for many years. The only transactions were occasional share redeployments caused by death. I noted down a few names and figures and went out again into the east-windy Edinburgh air.

Ferguson, Roberts and Holburn, Solicitors to the Supreme Court, occupied offices in Queen Street. I took a tram this time, for it was getting late in the afternoon. I rang the bell at an old-fashioned inquiry counter and a girl who was quite a dish said she'd inquire if Mr David Holburn was in. He was, and would see me. Perhaps because of the Christian name I was expecting a young man. Mr David was at least seventy and crabby, peering severely at me over narrow spectacles. A coal fire burned in the grate by his desk.

'You're from the South, eh, Mr Panton?' he began. 'How can I help you?'

I explained my errand. At the mention of the Caledonian Spitsbergen Development Corporation he frowned.

'But I thought that was all settled,' he said testily. 'We're working on the conveyancing now.' He rustled through the papers on his desk with stiff, blue fingers.

I said, 'I'm sorry. I don't understand. You must be thinking of someone else. We heard nothing from you.'

'You're the people who wanted to make a holiday camp or some such affair up there?'

'Well, yes. A guesthouse actually. But I don't think we went into details in our letter.'

Mr David pressed a bell-push which sounded a deep raspberry in the outer office. The dish put her head round the door.

'Bring me in Calspit Five,' said Mr David, and turning to me, 'Who are you exactly, might I ask?'

I told him — Peregrine Potter, Limited, Travel Consultants. Holidays off the Beaten Track. He frowned again and gave the fire an irritable poke.

'You're nothing to do with Erskine Rogerson, then? Or these people in Germany?'

'Certainly not with any Mr Rogerson. We are associated with a travel agency in Berlin like ourselves. Herr Randers is its head.'

'No, it wasn't a name quite like that. Something short and heathen. Never mind, we'll have it in a minute. You say you have had no dealings with Mr Rogerson?'

'None. We don't know the name. Who is he?'

Mr David didn't answer my question. He just said, 'Oh, you'll have to deal with *him*. Everyone does.'

The dish returned with a file — everything about the Spitsbergen business seemed bound up in files. Mr David dusted it with a red handkerchief before laying it carefully on his desk and opening it.

'Here we are,' he said. 'Verband Junger Pioniere.' He read it slowly without any attempt at German pronunciation. 'What would that mean in a Christian language?'

'Literally, League of Young Pioneers. Perhaps League of Young Explorers.'

'Oh, it does, does it? Well then, there's also a sort of badge with the word Spartapol. From the Greek, I presume.' He spelled it out. 'The letter is signed by a Mr Bland. Or rather, a Dr Bland.'

'Not our man,' I said. 'What does he say?'

Mr David looked up over his spectacles. 'I'm afraid I'm not in the habit of reading my correspondence to any individual that cares to inquire.'

'I'm sorry. I didn't mean it that way.'

'Very well, Mr Panton. I accept your good faith. I can tell you that Dr Bland and his association or whatever it is wish to acquire the deeds to the Krossfjorden territories owned by the Caledonian Spitsbergen Development Corporation. The intention is to set up some form of recreation camp. They have made an agreeably handsome offer and I have been instructed by the shareholders to accept it subject to the approval of the Norwegian authorities.'

'I see. Were there any other offers?'

'You are very busy, Mr Panton. There were one or two, including one from the Norwegian government, who had already acquired the other territories of the Corporation. This offer, however, was considerably more generous. Indeed, Mr Panton, it was exceptionally generous.'

I opened my mouth to speak but Mr David continued, as if defending himself, 'You must understand, Mr Panton, that the shareholders in this company have had not a penny for over twenty years. The proceeds of the first sale scarcely paid the costs of a fresh mineralogical survey that was made five or six years ago. They are mostly very old people now, living in much reduced circumstances. This transaction will be in the nature of a windfall which will bring much comfort.'

'I suppose it will,' I brooded. There didn't seem to be much left for us.

Mr David closed the file. 'It would appear that your own application, Mr Panton, has been somewhat overlooked. For this I must apologize. It was possibly the confusion of your associate's name — Rander is it? — with that of Dr Bland. But in any case you would have been too late. The present negotiations began many months ago.'

I nodded and prepared to go.

Mr David said, 'My advice would be to approach Mr Erskine Rogerson. He has been closely concerned with the disposal of all these old properties.' Without saying as much, he indicated the interview was at an end.

There was time for one more call before the evening plane. It was to the granite fortress of the *Scotsman*, where an old chum of mine called Jessie Blackwell, a rather solemn girl, worked on the Woman's Page. While we drank tea from thick cups she sent to the library for the cuttings on the Caledonian Spitsbergen Development Corporation.

'What is it?' she asked. 'I never heard of it.'

'It was before your time, luv.' I stirred my tea with a yellow H.B.

A scowling boy brought a faded orange folder the size of a long envelope. Mostly it contained only brief references cut out and pasted on to slips of copy paper. But there was one big half page piece by a Special Representative, no less, complete with little maps, tables of figures, and even a smudgy photograph of someone in a cowboy hat. The date, rubber-stamped across the top, was 13 OCT 33.

There wasn't time to study it properly before the plane went, much less make notes. Jess was busy on the phone. On the impulse I folded it and slipped it into my pocket. It was a bit of a lousy trick but I would post it back as soon as I had had it copied.

Somewhere over the Solway Firth I smoothed the cutting out and had another look. The style was pretty ponderous. It was understood that, your representative had reason to believe, etc. But the facts were all there, including a potted history of Spitsbergen, from discovery by Barents (1596) through literary allusions (Lord Dufferin: *Letters from High Latitudes*) to Scottish tics (somewhat tenuous).

I skipped on to the Flotation of the Caledonian Spitsbergen Development Corporation. Group of far-sighted Scottish businessmen … surveys … acquisition of lands and mineral rights … gypsum, marble, haematite … odd place names, half-Scotch, half-Norwegian, like Knoxtoppen and Holyroodhamna. At first operations succeeded; then came disappointment. The marble weathered, the gypsum petered out, the iron ore was elusive. A little table of declining figures.

But confidence that setbacks were only temporary. Engagement of a new consultant, the famous American mining engineer and Arctic pioneer, Mr Harry Williams. Rich rewards were still to be reaped from this far-off, severe land, said Mr Williams. It was his likeness which gazed out levelly from the picture, or what was visible of his likeness under the huge, high-crowned hat. He looked like the sheriff in an early Western, or something out of Walt Whitman.

Well, everything must have ground to a standstill not much later. The best-laid schemes, etc. It was dispiriting, like reading stuff written early in the war and knowing now the dreary years that lay in wait for the brave optimists who wrote it and read it.

CHAPTER FIVE

Peregrine was busy and harassed when I got back to the office. I reported briefly to him, wrote to Randers with what information I had, and on the way home dropped in to the public library to look up Erskine Rogerson.

It sounded the sort of name that ought to be in *Who's Who*. It was. William Erskine Rogerson, *b.* 1897, s. of late Surg. Capt. Erskine Erskine Rogerson, C.S.I., R.I.N., of Pittenweem, Fife, and Lady Kirsten Rogerson (*q.v.*). *Educ.* Fettes College and Peterhouse, Cambridge. Served 1915-18, Royal Naval Division, and 1939-45 (Cdr. R.N.V.R.). Mentioned in dispatches, 1918. C.B.E. 1944; Order of St Olav (Norway) 1945. Has taken part in numerous expeditions to Arctic regions. Clubs: Travellers' and Royal Automobile. Address: c/o Lloyd's Bank, Cox's & King's Branch.

A true pillar of the Establishment, I reflected. I wrote to him care of Cox's & King's.

In the days that followed, Peregrine's interest in Spitsbergen seemed to have vanished completely. I knew this trait of old. In routine matters he was methodical and energetic; the thought of a task left overnight would make him positively uneasy. But his few pet pie-in-the-sky projects were different; they would be indulged lavishly while he had the time and inclination, then shelved for months on end. If it hadn't been for the Mystery Caller, I doubt if Peregrination 22 would have been heard of again that year.

What made this episode so maddening was that both Peregrine and I should have been out of the office at the same time. Half an hour earlier or half an hour later and one of us would have been there when the Mystery Caller called.

'What did he look like?' I asked Dim Doreen for the third time.

'I told you. He was sort of, well, funny. Sort of foreign, you know. Yes, definitely a foreigner.'

'He had an accent?'

'Yes a sort of accent. Like a German only more like an American really.'

'What did he say?'

'Like I told you. He said, "I am interested in your expedition number 22." I said, "Oh yes, Peregrination 22." He said, "May I speak to someone about it, please?" Well, I knew you and Mr Potter were dealing with that one yourselves, so I said could he come back a bit later. Then Mrs Windern called across that it was all off.' She darted an accusing look across the office.

Mrs Windern flushed, which made her look even more like an overblown peony than usual. She was a professionally cheerful divorcee keeping a daughter at a goodish school and herself as chic as possible. She went in for tightish tailored costumes, roses at the bosom, and heady perfumes.

'I said it was off for this year,' she corrected. 'I didn't say it was cancelled altogether. I didn't want the client to have to come back for nothing, that was all.'

'You didn't ask him to leave a name and address?'

'To tell the truth, it was on the tip of my tongue, but he seemed to lose all interest. It was almost as if he were … *relieved* about it. Wasn't he, Doreen?'

'That's true,' said Dim Doreen, reluctantly backing up Mrs Windern.

'Naturally I asked him if he would be interested another year, and he said he would call again, perhaps. Then he went out.'

'You didn't ask him how he came to know about it?'

'I'm afraid not.' Mrs Windern pursed her lips in self-reproach.

'Did you notice anything else about him?'

'Only his glasses. I do remember noticing his glasses were rather unusual. Not the frames or anything. But the lenses themselves were tinted a very light green. Quite unusual, I thought. Distinctive, you know.'

'Perhaps it was friend Dancer in disguise,' I said. 'Trying to find out what's under the counter.'

The joke fell flat. The business was as mystifying as it was maddening. How *could* anyone have known about Peregrination 22? It wasn't in the brochure and never had been.

'Who gets proof copies?' I asked Peregrine.

'Just a few opposite numbers in the trade. Mainly in America.'

'Would Randers have had one?'

'Yes, he would. Incidentally, has he replied yet?'

'No.'

'Well, get on to him on the telephone. Find out what's happening and if this could be anything to do with him.'

Continental phone calls were a rare luxury *chez* Potter. The Mystery Caller incident had served not only to revive Peregrine's interest in Svalbard — it had made him hopping mad as well. He couldn't bear the idea of proof copies of *Peregrinations* reaching the public.

Randers was no longer at the Berlin number on his letterhead. An aggrieved voice didn't know where he had gone. That was no obstacle to the persistent German telephone system. At half past three the Continental Exchange came on the line again, and a moment later I was through.

'Ah, it is Colin. How are you?' But the voice seemed a bit subdued.

'Did you get my letter? Who are these young pioneers or Spartans or whatever they are? Have you contacted them?'

'Colin, I must tell you. I am speaking from the Spartapol office now. When I saw you I did not know that they were already making approaches to Edinburgh.'

'Well, who are they? And what do they plan to do?'

'Col, they are my associates in the sheem now. When you did not seem very anxious we have joined forces together.'

Bonk! That was a bit of a startler. I said, 'We're very anxious. In fact we're more anxious than ever. Why the hell didn't you say that you had other parties lined up?'

'I am sorry. At the time nothing was definite, you knao.' Randers's o-sounds had a kind of strangled nasal quality, evident even over the telephone. 'When I am getting back here they are wanting to get on very quickly.'

'Does that mean we're dropped?'

'Nao, nao, Col. I am sure there will be room for all.'

'And another thing — did you give anyone our brochure? You know, *Peregrinations*? The proof copy sent out at Christmas?'

Silence.

Then: 'I think not. Why?'

'Someone came in today, asking for the Spitsbergen tour that we were still planning. It's not in the final copies.'

'I do not think it can have been me.'

Peregrine had heard my raised voice and come in. He was making signs and mouthing.

I said into the phone, 'Well, we'll see you up there — one of us — as arranged. Next month.'

Another silence.

Then: 'Col, I must go earlier now than we said. I must go on the first sailing of the steamer from Tromsø at the end of this month. I am sorry —'

'Just a minute.' I put my hand over the mouthpiece and told Peregrine.

'We'll go too,' he said decisively.

I uncovered the mouthpiece. 'We'll go too. Which way are you getting to Tromsø?'

'Through Stockholm and Narvik, I expect, but…'

'We'll meet in Tromsø, then,' I said. 'Bye now.' It was impossible to argue coherently with Peregrine standing over me. I looked up at him. 'The old double-dealer. What do you know about *that*?'

According to the shipping company's leaflet the steamship *Bellsund* left Tromsø for the first voyage of the season to Spitsbergen on June 24th, which was just eight days away. Peregrine wired immediately for a reservation.

'We'll fix the rest tomorrow,' he said. I knew that he also meant we'd decide who went then, and that he hoped I would volunteer.

I tried to weigh it up that evening. There was still no word from my agent. I was uneasy about leaving London for three weeks. On the other hand, I hadn't had a holiday for three years. A moth butted drowsily against the table lamp on my desk. Out in the square the trees were heavy with foliage, and as the day's dust and fumes diminished the air had that faint, disturbing fragrance of early summer, big city. It was just a year since the Jane affair was in its first casual rapture. For some reason I remembered the night we'd been disturbed by a metallic crash outside the window. Jane, curious, had padded over to the window.

'Come back,' I'd said irritably. Her little white bottom was shining palely in the gloom.

'Come and look,' she'd urged.

It was a little old vintage car, painted primrose, that often stood in the square. The front axle must have broken completely. The car had lurched down like a stricken animal on its knees. The owner and his pals stood around, shocked out of their usual loudness. In the end they got it jacked up, but we didn't stay to watch.

Next morning I told Peregrine I'd go to Spitsbergen for him. He was pleased and let his pleasure show, now that I'd decided. He set about fixing the travel straight away. I was to follow the Peregrination 22 route: by air to Oslo and on to Trondheim; coastal steamer from Trondheim to Tromsø for the sake of the spectacular scenery. But second post brought a letter, at last, from the legendary Erskine Rogerson. It was typed in blue on thick white paper. The address was Norwegian, and long-winded. He was sorry but we had just missed him in London. He wouldn't be back there again until August. In the meantime he would be glad to see us in Norway should we be over there at all. His place was just off the Bergen-Oslo railway.

Peregrine shrugged and amended the bookings he'd made in the morning. The obvious course now, he explained, was to catch the express steamer across the North Sea to Bergen, go by train to Rogerson's, continue the rail journey to Oslo, and then fly all the way up to Tromsø in order to make up lost time.

'Under the circumstances,' he said, 'it would be silly not to see the man. You'll miss the coastal steamer trip, which is rather a pity. But I can use the cabin booking — they're hard to come by at this time of the year and friend Dancer had finally decided he wants to go on the Lofotens trip. So it's an ill wind.'

CHAPTER SIX

'What are people wearing in the Arctic this year?'

The elegant youth in Peter Jones's smiled warily.

'Ha, ha.'

'No, really,' I said stonily.

He thought. 'Would that be like for skiing?'

'I suppose so.'

'Well, that's all been put away now. End of March that goes. I mean there's no call for it in summer, is there?' His hand circled in tentative embracement of the summer display of bullfight posters, underwater swimming gear and straw figures in boxer shorts.

He called after me, 'They might have some duffel coats in overcoats,' but I'd decided to travel light. After all, it probably wouldn't be any colder than Aldeburgh, and I could take Aldeburgh.

I bought a pale-blue plastic mac in a little pouch, in case of rain, and a blazer of rough hopsack that looked as if it would keep its shape fairly well. In the W. H. Smiths across the road I looked through the paperback thrillers without much luck, but noticed — and bought — James Fisher's Penguin on Bird Recognition, the one dealing with seabirds. Spitsbergen sounded an ornithological sort of place. I could improve my mind.

Twenty-four hours later I stood on the sun deck of the Newcastle-Bergen boat as she drove down the sulphurous Tyne and out to sea. At the estuary mouth was a sudden, mournful patch of yellow sand, brightly lit by the afternoon sun. People were sitting on deck chairs. Children in bathing costumes, knee-deep in the grey tide, waved as we passed. A minute later the ship rose slightly to the first swell of the sea. I went in search of tea, wanting to relish to myself the luxury of having nothing, absolutely nothing, to do. No work. No overdue script. No niggling inner voice suggesting I ought to Write Something. Not even any washing up. It was good to be alone.

So there, of course, was friend Dancer putting down his teacup, smiling uncertainly and half-rising from his seat. I'd had one session with him in the office when Peregrine had been out, and I'd talked to him on the phone at least three times as he struggled with the awful problem of where to go for his annual expedition. He had a kindly oval face surmounted by greying hair which was still cut exactly as it must have been when he was in the fourth form, even to a jaunty little plume sticking up from the crown. He also had an incongruously boyish voice impediment — though he must have been approaching his fifties — combined with a way of pronouncing his 'l' sounds so they sounded more like r's, in a way impossible to indicate in print. He shook my hand limply.

'An unexpected pleasure. Would you like some tea?' Then he thought of something and frowned. Clearly the vexed arrangements for his trip still occupied his mind. 'This doesn't mean you want your cabin back, does it?'

'What cabin? Of course, the one on the coastal steamer.' I smiled reassuringly. 'No, no. I'm going on by train from Bergen. Our paths diverge.'

He smiled too. 'It's silly of me, I know, but it has been such a muddle this year — not your fault, of course…'He looked sad again. 'When you haven't much else to think about, quite unimportant things t-take over.'

I felt a twinge of sympathy. He had certainly earned his holiday, the worry and work he'd put into deciding on it. In the end the decision was so tardy that he had incurred several additional expenses: more than one cable across the North Sea, and now a stage by amphibian plane from Bergen to Trondheim in order to retrieve two days lost by starting off late.

'The b-bank were quite cross,' he was saying. 'They'd just got me all my Icelandic kroner when I told them I wanted Norwegian instead.'

We had dinner together as well. I found I didn't mind friend Dancer at all. Once over a formidable shyness he could be amusing. He told me he lived in Brighton alone except for an old housekeeper who had been one of his mother's maids. He had a private income from holdings in the big firm which twenty years before had taken over the family business, and he had never had a real job. Dramatic criticism he wrote for one of the Brighton papers brought in a guinea or two but was more important for the slight position it gave him in the town. He passed on some mildly bitchy green-room gossip from new shows which had passed through on their way to London. His anxiety not to miss any of the important try-outs, he explained, had a lot to do with his vacillation.

'That's why I left so late when I did decide,' he added ruefully. 'I couldn't bear to miss that p-play of Norman Hunter's. And I so wanted to be back for the eighth. That's a première, you know.'

When we said good-night he said, shyly again, 'I enj-joyed meeting you. I always travel on my own. I'm q-quite used to it, but I usually find the first day lonely. It's been a good start this year, th-thanks to you.'

The awful thing was that I saw it could be me in fifteen or twenty years' time, the way I was drifting.

Bergen, in the morning, was blanketed in heavy rain. It fell absolutely vertically, steadily, without pause or variation. A taxi swished me from the customs sheds to the station, where the high brown coaches of the Oslo train awaited.

CHAPTER SEVEN

The journey was interminable. As the train climbed away from Bergen into the mountains the windows misted over. When I rubbed a patch clear with a newspaper I saw desolate country encrusted still in the cracks and crevices with deposits of winter snow. Sometimes there was a sudden dizzy glimpse of a fjord thousands of feet below. Well, hundreds. Other times the wooden walls built to protect the line from drifts closed in and all view was shut off.

I lunched early, mainly from boredom. An hour after I'd wended my way back to my seat we reached the halt for Rogerson's place. There was a scatter of timber buildings, a waiting bus, the bright-painted cars of a little funicular railway that climbed even higher into the mountains; but not at first any sign of Rogerson. He emerged a few moments later from what was evidently the post office.

My first impression was that we probably wouldn't get on very well. He was a very big man, not only tall and broad but heavy, too, with a ruddy face and massive eyebrows; one of nature's commanding officers. But his smile was friendly enough. He said, 'It's awfully good of you to make this detour. I expect you're feeling a bit Bolshie about it.'

His voice was warmer than I had expected, without that military edge to it. I murmured not at all, it was a pleasure, something like that. Rogerson took my bag and led the way to a Land Rover parked outside the post office. We drove along a main road, steep and twisty but well-metalled, only turning off on to a lesser, bumpy track for the last mile or two.

He talked briefly of the tedium of the train journey, the weather (still dull), the advantages and disadvantages of a Land Rover. In profile his head had a leonine massiveness — I wasn't surprised when he told me later that the Norwegians sometimes took him for Churchill. The hands that held the steering wheel were large and pink, with prominent veins on the back. In appearance he might have been anything between fifty and sixty-five.

As he turned the truck over a little wooden bridge and into the courtyard of a low, steep-roofed house he said, 'This is my place. It belonged to Quisling once. The Norwegians let me buy it afterwards.' He never expanded on this information or volunteered any reason for living in Norway.

The house was one for *Homes and Gardens*. One big room with varnished pine floors. Profusion of light-coloured rugs. Low tweedy chairs. Pictures on the walls. Through wide windows, a view over a misty, rainswept lake. It was like a troll king's palace.

Although it was nearly July, an armful of logs smouldered in an open fireplace. Rogerson gave them a kick, bade me sit down, and said he'd see about some coffee. I took a closer look at the pictures. They were all modern, all landscapes, and mostly very good. I was in front of an Anne Redpath when Rogerson came back.

'Galloway, near Newton Stewart,' he said, and took me on a curious topographical tour of the rest of the collection, identifying the subject of every picture but only occasionally mentioning the name of the painter. He listened attentively to my mumbled comments without offering any critical views of his own, not even a simple 'I like it' or 'Charming, isn't it?'

Finally we came to a shadowy alcove containing a big bureau, and above it a picture I hadn't noticed before.

'You ought to see this one,' said Rogerson, and switched on a lamp standing on the bureau. 'It's Longyear, up in Svalbard where you're going. But I doubt if you'll ever see it like that.'

Momentarily, I was disappointed, for the picture was not a painting at all, but a half-plate photograph. It was taken in the Arctic night, looking across a broad snowy valley. On the near side was a double line of large buildings, their lighted windows shining brightly. Across the far side were similar buildings, now dwarfed by the great shadow-streaked hillside that rose behind. Fragile chains of light indicated roads joining the two colonies; and half-way up the distant slope was another cluster of lights with a dark line descending from it to the valley floor. The sky was a flat neutral shade.

'One of the mines,' said Rogerson prosaically, pointing to the isolated lights on the hillside. 'They are really just tunnels into the side of the mountain. That's a cableway to take the coal down to the bottom of the valley. They dig most of the coal in the winter. Three shifts round the clock. It's night all the time, of course.'

'I think it's one of the most exciting pictures I've ever seen.' Rogerson looked at me with new interest. He was about to say something when the coffee arrived, brought by a middle-aged woman in maid's apron and cap. She stood the tray on a low table by the fire and vanished again.

'Perhaps we'd better get down to business,' said Rogerson. He lowered himself into an armchair and poured the coffee. 'Let me declare my interest. Spitsbergen is an old love of mine. The first time I went there was nearly thirty years ago. I've been back a good few times, too. I was even there in the war for a while. I know the place pretty well.'

He drank some coffee. 'Lately I've been acting as a sort of go-between in the disposal of some of these old British concessions. They were mostly pretty worthless, you know. Deeds to a lot of snow and ice. Well, we've been quietly selling the whole lot back to the Norwegian government. All at high level — Foreign Office blessing and so on. Confidentially, neither side was anxious to see the properties come on to the open market in case the Russians made a bid for them. Which they could have done quite legally, of course.'

I nodded sagely.

'As you probably know they've got a couple of pretty big settlements up there already. Nothing against that. It was just that … well, we didn't want to see them get any more at this particular time. Anyway, there's just this one lot left, the one you're interested in.'

'Were interested in,' I corrected.

'Why?'

'Our idea seems rather to have got lost.' I described briefly what had been happening, finishing with the interview with the Edinburgh solicitors.

Rogerson listened carefully. At the end he said, 'I'm afraid I can't help you a great deal since you aren't actually in the market for the land yourselves. The other side are, you see.'

'Yes, I suppose so.'

'But I don't see why your little scheme shouldn't fit in with theirs.'

'That's what I'll have to try and fix.'

'Unless' — he grinned — 'they want to dash about with no clothes on all day. In which case your people might be in the way.'

I blinked.

'I wouldn't know about that. What is this Spartapol exactly? I heard it was some sort of youth club, and that's all.'

Rogerson fished amongst a pile of magazines on a stool by his side. 'It started off as a German idea called the Verband Junger Pioniere. The aim was to run a camp in the Arctic and since Spitsbergen is an officially neutral zone they hoped to be able to have youngsters from both East and West Germany. But I gather they found this would be easier if they threw the thing open generally and made it a European stunt.'

He found what he was looking for amid the magazines and passed me a leaflet printed in German, French and English.

'The fellow Bland you mentioned came to see me,' said Rogerson. 'He seemed quite a decent sort. He left me that paper. It's only a preliminary thing but it has the main idea there.'

I was busy looking at the list of 'Patrons' that headed the paper. It included a couple of German princelings, one legendary industrialist, a former French prime minister, and from Britain — well, not such a surprising eminence. It was rather in his line, this sort of thing. I skimmed over the text. Spartapol was the name of the proposed camp — there was some guff about recapturing the spirit of ancient Sparta — and by extension, the name of the camp now seemed to apply to the whole movement.

'I find it a bit alarming,' I said finally.

'How?'

'Well, you know, Strength-through-Joyish.'

'I should have thought it wasn't so very different from our own Outward Bound scheme.'

'There you are.' It was a silly thing to say, and I knew it straight away.

Rogerson went flinty. 'I happen to have quite a lot to do with the Outward Bound movement.'

'Sorry. Said wrong thing.'

'You're entitled to your views. I happen to think there's nothing wrong in youngsters getting a bit of fresh air and hard living. Do them good.'

'Are you satisfied it could be nothing more?'

'You mean some secret military affair? Heavens, no. The Germans are past that kind of thing. Hate military service, you know. Won't do it if they can help it.' He heaved himself from his chair and looked out of the broad window. Against the light his great tufted eyebrows were like horns. 'But I will admit I'd like to know something more about the scheme, if only because I feel a sort of — well, responsibility about Spitsbergen.'

He was almost embarrassed now. 'It's a strange place, a very beautiful place. It's more than that — it's something very special, which ought to be kept very special. I went up there for the first time when I was nineteen, and it has exercised a spell over me ever since.'

He sat down again. 'Frankly, I'd have liked this last parcel of land to stay in British hands, or failing that go to the Norwegians. But I'm only an adviser in these matters. The final decision rests with the corporation, and you can't blame them for selling to the highest bidder.'

I ummed in agreement.

'Unfortunately, time is short. Both sides are pressing to complete the deal as soon as possible. I'd go up there myself but I'm supposed to be going later in the season when the Governor's back. Old friend of mine. In Majorca at the moment, of all places.'

He looked at me speculatively as if weighing up my reliability. 'Look, quite apart from your own interest I'd be very glad if you'd keep your eyes open on my behalf. I mean, if there's anything at all that worries you about these Spartapol people…' He paused. 'If you wouldn't mind.'

'Not at all,' I said automatically.

'Just let me know, and I can always hold things up, you see.'

'I'd be glad to.' I felt a curious onset of responsibility as if I'd been picked for jury service.

If I were to catch the next train on to Oslo it was time to go. 'I'm afraid it's a bit of a stopper,' said Rogerson.

He drove me to the halt. On the way he talked with sudden loquacity about the Arctic. Of his first trips with university expeditions in the Long Vacs, to Spitsbergen, Edge Island, Greenland. Of Gino Watkins and Martin Lindsay and Augustine Courtauld and all the other young lions he'd known and accompanied. Of their brave, stiff-upper-lip exploits and extraordinary fortitude. Of rolling, seasick voyages in stinking sealers. Of hands black with frostbite, and toothache a thousand miles from a dentist. Of his wartime return to Spitsbergen to evacuate the settlements. Sailing up the familiar fjords in a destroyer. The silent miners and their women packing to go. The pall of smoke from burning installations as they sailed away.

He ended with a touch of evocative description, of his one visit to the elusive church-spire island of Jan Mayen, rising from the Greenland Sea like a mirage, with silence all around. This in the little refreshment room by the track over a couple of brandies and the statutory sandwiches. As he talked I felt again a quickening of the pulse that I had felt when I looked at the framed photograph of Longyear City under the long night. The feeling lasted me through dinner and might have lasted longer if the train hadn't exceeded Rogerson's worst expectations and shuffled into Oslo's clinically clean station past midnight.

CHAPTER EIGHT

My hotel was a tall thin block in a business street now dark and deserted. No one seemed to be on duty except a manager drinking beers with a couple of cronies in the minute foyer. He showed me to a room on the seventh floor and said did I want a drink. Apparently I couldn't have spirits because of the licensing laws. I settled for a glass of Madeira and a slice of cake, and asked for a call at seven the next morning. At least I'm pretty sure I did. I certainly meant to. Maybe it was the wine, which was rather agreeable in a lush kind of way, very sweet and strong and presumably fortified to the hilt. Anyway, I slept like a dog. When I woke, the light was pouring strongly through the heavy net curtains, and street noises floated up from below. I dredged around under the pillow for my watch.

Twenty to nine! Getting up has never been a strong point, but this once I bounded up, pulled some clothes on, and shot downstairs two at a time. The clock in the foyer chimed the three-quarters as I arrived in a heap at the office. The same manager was there. Perhaps he was the owner. 'No one woke me,' I screamed. 'What's the big idea? Now I've missed my plane.'

The manager tilted his head and looked at the blackboard on the wall by his cubby-hole, chalked with call instructions. Number 17, Kl. 7.45. Number 25, Kl. 8.00, kaffe. My room was number 28, and it wasn't featured.

'I'm sure I asked you last night,' I said lamely.

'It seems not.' His English and his equanimity were equally infuriating. 'What time plane you wanted?'

'The plane north. Eight o'clock at the terminal, nine at the airport.'

'Nine take-off?'

'Yes, I think so.'

'Too late now, anyway. Unless she is delayed.' He dialled a number on the telephone and spoke rapidly in Norwegian, then masked the mouthpiece with his hand. 'No, she's on time. Will I tell them you can't make it?'

I nodded miserably.

'It's okay,' said the manager, ringing off. 'I told them you were sick. Otherwise you'd have a no-show fine to pay.'

'What do I do now?' I could hardly speak.

'There's another plane tomorrow, I guess.' He unfolded a leaflet. 'Certainly, yes. Trondheim, Bodø, every day, Sundays the same. You must go along to the terminal and fix a reservation.'

'Thank you.' But I was scowling. I went up in the slow little lift kicking the door with rage. What a stupid, idiotic trick! Now the whole trip was ruined. I wasn't even sure if I could still get to Tromsø in time to catch the boat. If I did, it would still be a hot and bothered business. Suddenly it was the most important thing in the world to get to Spitsbergen.

After some breakfast I had myself directed to the air terminal. At first they weren't very encouraging. Next day was Sunday and though there was the regular morning landplane as far as Bodø there was no seaplane service on to Tromsø. Monday there would be one, but Monday was leaving it awfully late. Any hold-up and I would miss the Spitsbergen sailing. The best thing, thought the clerk, thumbing a massive looseleaf timetable, would be to take the Sunday flight to Bodø and catch the coastal steamer on to Tromsø. It wouldn't arrive until late afternoon the next day but the risk of delay was less.

While I was pondering over this information the clerk brightened. He had remembered something.

'Yes, excuse me,' he beamed. 'Of course, you may go up tonight on the Midnight Sun flight.'

'*Tonight*?'

'Yes, yes. Every Saturday in the season we have special excursion trip. For the tourists, you know. They fly up to Bodø, see the Midnight Sun, spend a few hours above the Arctic Circle, fly back. Very popular. But it's a regular scheduled flight. You don't *have* to come back same night.'

'Ah, but is there a connection on to Tromsø?'

'Ja, of course. Shall I try for a reservation?'

'I suppose so. What time does it get there?' I was still uncertain. There was sure to be a catch somewhere.

The clerk had been reaching for the phone. He let his hand rest on it, waiting blankly. I became aware of impatient noises behind me, someone trying to push past. A voice was aimed at the clerk. '*Til Tromsø i dag.*' Something like that, rather peremptory.

I said quickly, 'Yes, try for that flight, will you please?' and glared round.

The man who had been trying to bypass me shrugged and dropped back again, keeping his attention on the clerk. The thing I noticed about him straight away was the green tints of his glasses. Mrs Windern's description of the Mystery Caller was still vivid, but of course, it was only a coincidence. Millions of people have tinted lenses.

I stood squarely against the counter and spread my hands on it to try and exclude him physically. The clerk was hanging on his phone, waiting for an answer with practised, vacant patience, as if he'd switched himself off to save the battery. The man dropped back a bit more, chafing with impatience —

it was like a cloud round his head — and looking up and down the counter to see if there was anywhere else he could get in.

Apart from the green specs there wasn't anything obvious to distinguish him. He might have been any bald, middle-aged European between Sweden and, say, North Italy. But taking a closer look, as I did now, there was a certain impression of strength and determination. It wasn't so much the tightness of his mouth or the set of his head or the firmness of his tanned skin as the realization that he hadn't even looked at me. He wasn't interested. I was only a back, in the way.

The clerk was speaking. He could get me on the big plane to Bodø all right. The seaplane on to Tromsø was fully booked but I could go on the wait list. There was a good chance of a seat turning up by the time we got to Bodø. I thanked him and accepted. Even to be able to start out on the journey was good for peace of mind. As I turned to go, Greeneyes was already in my place, cutting off the clerk's goodbye. '*Til Tromsø i dag?*'

I enjoyed mooning around Oslo the rest of the day. The sun shone, the air was bright and clear, the girls were inviting in summer frocks and bare limbs, the long trams hissed and swivelled through the streets. I looked forward to the midnight flight. The clerk had given me a leaflet which I read over a lunch time beer. It began with a Shakespeare quote and continued in heady prose. Arctic Norway, it seemed, was a favoured haunt of sportive British dukes and lords. I hoped it would be sportive for me.

CHAPTER NINE

The waiter worked out his tip to two places of decimals.

I paid, collected my things, and strolled along to the terminal. It was one of those matchless Scandinavian evenings of warm luminosity. The crowds drifted placidly along the pavements, window-gazing and each-other-gazing. The whiff of small cigars hung in the air.

At the terminal the midnight sun travellers waited expectantly, hung with Leicas and nylon raincoats and Pan-Am satchels. They regarded me speculatively. I hoped I looked like a sportive duke or lord. We boarded the dark-blue coach and drove out through scattered suburbs. The tall blocks of flats stood crisply against the blue sky the way our own housing schemes do in the architects' drawings but never in execution. Twice we passed running tracks laid out in the grounds. Round one of them plodded a dozen earnest young Vikings.

The tourists began to come to life, chattering amongst themselves. They hadn't been sure whether to make the trip or not. But the man in the American Express had said it was a must. Don't miss up on the Midnight Sun trip, he'd said, whatever else you miss up. The plane was waiting at the airport. A DC-6. Why, it had four engines, the tourists reassured themselves. They'd been half expecting an old biplane or something. I looked around the airport lounge. It was really no surprise to recognize Greeneyes, standing near the departure gate. Already I felt that in some way our journeys were linked.

They called us to the plane. In the usual irrational scramble to board first he was way in front and I was way behind. By the time I reached the step-ladder he had vanished. As I entered the plane I saw him sitting in the little first-class cabin at the rear. For the first time our eyes met — or rather my eyes and his pale green lenses, subtly screening the identity behind them. He looked at me briefly and then away, still uninterested.

The flight was not quite as spectacular as the leaflet claimed, but nearly. We flew over mile after mile of splintered granite slopes broken by streams and deep valleys. The sun sank low over the sea to the west, filling the cabin with gold and purple lights. Between intakes of nature I sipped Scotch from a celluloid glass and skipped through *Look*, *Life*, *See*, *Paris-Match*, and a dull periodical about airlines. The magazines were in a rack at the back of the cabin and every time I went to change them I could steal a look at Greeneyes. Mostly he seemed asleep or sunk in a motionless reverie. At Trondheim, where we landed for half an hour, he stood on the tarmac aloof and alone.

Two of the travellers were pretending to board the DC-6 again, luggage in hand, while a third man — a little fellow with a fringe of beard — busily filmed them with a cine camera. The actors were evidently American, and a curious pair. He was old and a bit infirm, with a head that hung forward from his body like a big bird's. She was large and lurid, with extravagantly red hair, Texas boots, and a laugh that rang out brassily. As we watched, an official trotted up shaking his head and pointing. It was forbidden to take photographs, as the airport was also a military field.

'Okay,' I heard the woman say. 'We got it anyway.' Then they ambled away from the plane, her voice yapping over the top of the little old man's murmured bass. The cameraman tailed after them, putting his gear back into leather cases.

Bodø was an airport being carved out. The big earth-movers stood around on the edges of great brown scars on the landscape. Outside the passenger buildings a signpost pointed to New York, Los Angeles, Tokyo. A bus waited for onward passengers, and taxis to take the trippers to restaurants in the hills.

Greeneyes looked as if he were trying for a taxi instead of waiting for the bus. A battered Dodge drew up, labelled 'Drosje'. I suppose it's the same word as Droshky. On the spur of the moment I sidled up as Greeneyes began to climb in.

'Are you going into the town? Perhaps we could share the cab.'

The glasses flashed briefly at me. Greeneyes made no reply for a moment, then shrugged and moved over to the far side of the seat.

We bumped off along an unmetalled road. I said, 'It was a fascinating flight, wasn't it?' He nodded and stared out of the window. Bodø seemed to be a boom town, springing up all around. I tried again. 'Are you staying here or going on?'

'Bitte?'

I repeated the question in German. Greeneyes jerked his head.

'Further,' he grunted. 'Further.'

A minute later the droshky stopped. It hadn't been a very long ride. Greeneyes clambered out and paid the driver. I proffered two kroner. He took one, nodded again, and walked decisively off. I lingered perhaps a second. It was a kind of shanty-town street, raw and new, mainly wooden huts. The smell of smoking fish pervaded the air and even at midnight the sky was light though also nocturnal, like midnight blue watered down.

I turned to follow Greeneyes and saw too late what he was up to. He was disappearing into a hut marked with the triple crown motif of Scandinavian Airlines. It was the seaplane office and he was after any spare seat there might be on the Tromsø flight.

Inside the hut a sleepy official was checking a typed list while Greeneyes hovered over him. A man in uniform with wings and bands on his sleeve stood by, cleaning out his nails with a penknife: the captain of the plane, I guessed.

It was my turn now to stand second in line, quivering with impatience. The official nodded to himself, detached a leaf from Greeneyes' airline ticket and handed him a boarding card. Greeneyes turned and side-stepped out, past me. His face was impassive.

The official looked up. He had pale gingery hair and a ginger stubble on his chin.

I was on the wait list,' I said. 'I hope there's a place for me. Panton.' I spelled it.

The pencil poised over the list, found my name, marked it. 'I'm sorry, the plane is full.'

'But they said at Oslo there would almost certainly be a place.'

'I'm sorry. There's only one plane this time. It doesn't hold many persons. There have not been enough names on the wait list to have two planes.'

'But this is ridiculous! What do I do now?'

The official's eyes flicked behind me to the little queue that was forming. 'One minute, eh?' he said.

I stood to one side and waited while six, seven, eight more passengers collected their boarding cards. The Americans' cameraman collected three. As the last was ticked off the list the official looked up again. 'No luck,' he said cheerfully.

'Everyone came. I guess the plane is full.' He turned in confirmation to the captain, who nodded.

'Well *I've got* to get to Tromsø. It's important.'

'How soon?'

'By tomorrow evening.'

'Oh, you'll be all right. We have two planes tomorrow afternoon. Plenty of room.'

'That's all very well. They told me in Oslo I'd be able to get up now. What's the use of going on a wait list if no one gets on the plane?' I meant it to be a bit of a trap, and by and large it was.

'One person was fortunate.'

'Who? The man who came in here first?' There was a nod. 'Why him? Just because he got in here first. I was before him in Oslo.'

'Yeah, but he sent us a telegram before Oslo phoned us.'

'Well, I'd have done the same if I'd known. No one told me to.'

It was no good. The official was sympathetic, but no more. The captain put away his penknife. He was a rakish chap. 'I am very sorry, sir,' he said. 'I would wink at the regulations, you understand, and take you, if the freight was light. We always fly with one seat empty. But we have to carry an extra person already, you might say?'

The official smirked. The captain grinned. 'Not,' he added, 'that this poor man will see much of the journey.'

'He is a coffin,' said the official, anxious that I should share the joke.

'A corpus,' corrected the captain.

Very humorous. 'In that case,' I said sourly, 'couldn't he be the one to wait? After all, a day here or there won't make much difference to where he's going.'

Ah, no, sorry. They were sympathetic but inflexible. I went out and glared around. The line of huts ran down to the fjord, basking metallically in the low midnight sun. A couple of fishing boats were tied up at a jetty and out in the water floated an old Junkers tri-motor seaplane, square and venerable.

I wandered down towards the water's edge, then side-stepped instinctively into the shadows. Greeneyes stood a little way from a blue airline van parked by the jetty. He stood quite motionless, oblivious, head bent. As I watched, two men in overalls and airline caps struggled to unload a white coffin from the van. They lowered it with a bump on to a handcart and wheeled it down the jetty. As it passed Greeneyes he took the green spectacles off with a sudden gesture, then replaced them. When I thought about it afterwards it seemed almost like a salute.

I walked along the water's edge for perhaps a quarter of a mile until huts, quayside, and for that matter the whole town, petered out in damp sea-grass and cinders. When I got back the passengers were assembling for the flight. I sat on a baulk of wood and watched them go. The Junkers roared off with much noise, a yellow-painted speedboat tagging along in its wake. I wondered how to kill the next twelve hours. What *do* you do in a shanty town at 2 a.m.? What I did was to go back to the airport and doze on a settee under an S.A.S. blanket until it was time for breakfast.

CHAPTER TEN

Anxiously checking the coastal steamer schedules during the morning to make sure I would reach Tromsø in time, I made the discovery that I was about to rejoin the original Peregrination 22 timetable, the air-sea combination which Peregrine had wanted me to follow before we knew about the Rogerson detour. The northward-bound vessel due at noon was the very one I would have caught at Trondheim two days earlier. In other words, friend Dancer would be aboard. I looked forward to seeing him again. It would be rather a bore explaining how I had missed my connections, but he wasn't bad company and the charms of solitary travel were beginning to wear thin.

The boat came in on time. It was evidently the event of the day in Bodø. Crowds appeared from nowhere and lined the quayside. The people aboard returned the compliment, crowding the rails and waving. When the gangplanks came down they were jammed in a concerted rush to get on/off straight away. I waited until the worst was over before fighting my way aboard. There was no sign of Dancer. I set off on a squeezing-past, excusing-please exploration. I had an idea that the cabin — *my* cabin, it would have been — was A.5. I must have seen the number on the travel documents in the office and it had left a lingering association image of the A.5 trunk road where it undulates rather splendidly from Beds, into Northants. But the door to A.5 was locked. I went on my way, noting with dismay how few cabins there were and how many passengers. Another long day-night stretched ahead — the second running — and the only alternative resting place seemed to be a dismal sort of waiting room I found deep in the bowels of the ship, with leather benches along the walls and more leather benches wrapped round the fat ventilation shafts that joined floor and ceiling.

It was a dreary prospect. I wished desperately that I could have flown off safe and snug aboard the old Junkers, and cursed Greeneyes repetitively under my breath. At the same time it became increasingly urgent to find Dancer. I toiled along companion ways, dragged down by my grip, side-stepping past and bumping into people, looking for his gentle face and schoolboy haircut. But there were only peasant families seated in rows as they munched cheese sandwiches and shelled hard-boiled eggs. The saloon was packed and airless, the ship's office besieged by a small but patient crowd. I joined it and fretted for five minutes, then changed my mind. In the five minutes I did find out something, however. There was a typewritten cabin disposition pinned up by the door. A.5 was the right one. Indeed it was still in my name, which gave me the slight turn that you get whenever you see your name unexpectedly displayed.

I found a place at the deck rail. On the quayside the crowds were as thick as ever. Crates and boxes and big carboys in wicker baskets were being unloaded. Someone wheeled a shiny new motor bike down the gangplank. There was still time to go ashore. I wondered whether to wait until the next day and risk the plane. After all, the weather was fine. There was no reason to suppose anything could delay it. But then Dancer would surely turn up. Probably he had gone ashore himself to have a look at Bodø. It would have been easy to miss him in the crush. Having looked for him I felt a curious responsibility to stay, as if somehow he might know I was around and expect to find me.

At last we sailed. I leaned on my piece of rail for ten minutes watching the quayside and its thinning ranks of peasants recede, then sought out the saloon again. I fancied a cup of coffee and maybe a slice of dark brown goat's milk cheese like chocolate. But the place was crowded and the service desperate. I signalled ineffectually to the fat waitress in black.

'Hallo, there. Um, *please…*'

'Englishman, heh?' It was the man who was sitting opposite me, a great ruffian in a blue donkey-jacket. He was a huge man with a red face and a dark stubble. His hands rested on the table in front of him like dusty joints of meat.

I said, 'Yes.'

He shouted at the waitress and leaned conspiratorially forward. 'She'll bring it now. You see. Sure.'

'Thank you.' Stiffly.

'It's all right. She's a lousy woman. Where you going?'

'Up north, as a matter of fact.'

'Tromsø? Alta? Heh?'

'To Spitsbergen, actually.'

Donkey-jacket's eyes narrowed. 'What you going there for? Why in Jesus you want to go there?'

'I dunno, I just wanted to see the place, I suppose.'

Donkey-jacket pushed back his cap, scratching his bristly head. 'Yah, you don't want to go there. Nothing to do there in that dump. No women. No drinking. No fun. Why don't you go somewhere where's there fun?'

I shrugged. Donkey-jacket drank his beer. The glass looked absurdly small in his fist.

'You want a beer?' he demanded.

'No thanks. I've got the coffee coming.'

'Yah, go on. Have a beer. Do you good.'

'No thanks.' I shook my head like a maniac.

The coffee arrived. No cheese. Donkey-jacket ordered some more beer. I wished the hell he'd go away. But he was leaning forward again. 'Hamburg,' he said. 'Why don't you go to Hamburg? Plenty fun there. Plenty big dirty women. Yah, you go to Hamburg. Spitsbergen's no good. You on holiday?'

'In a way. Yes. Yes, I am.'

'You must be crazy. Have a beer.'

'No.'

'I tell you something. I got some schnapps. Good. Very strong. We can't drink it here. That lousy woman will make trouble. I'll see you after, heh?'

Not if I can help it, you won't, I thought. That would be nice, I said. I drank up the coffee and started to go.

Donkey-jacket reached out a restraining arm. It felt like a roadblock.

'You don't want to go to that dump,' he said softly. 'Go somewhere where there's fun.'

Looking back, the willies started then, though there was no particular cause for them yet. It was just that I was tired and a bit perplexed by Dancer's non-appearance. Also, Donkey-jacket gave me the creeps. I scuttled out of the saloon leaving a 2-kr. piece on the table to cover the cost of the coffee, and found cabin A.5 again. I gave the door-handle a vigorous jerk, expecting it still to be locked, only this time it yielded and I half-lurched inside.

'Yo?' said a woman's voice; at least that's how it sounded. She was a large woman in a white overall, a cabin maid or something. She looked up from packing clothes into a suitcase. The tie that dangled from her hand was the woven one that I remembered Dancer had been wearing when I last saw him. The suitcase was branded with the initials J.R.D.

'Oh, sorry. Do you know where Mr Dancer is?'

She shook her head, smiled, said something in Norwegian.

'Dancer. The man here?'

Stream of Norwegian. I wagged my head vacantly. She shrugged and looked around the cabin as if seeking some hidden interpreter. Dancer's suede shoes were placed neatly together on the floor. His toothbrush and flannel and a bottle of milk of magnesia stood on the little shelf over the washbasin. The woman folded his tie into his case, closed it, crossed the cabin to the door and beckoned me to follow her, locking up after us.

We went past the ship's office and stopped outside the next compartment. The woman knocked on the door and stood aside. As I went in she said something and then returned the way we'd come. It seemed to be an ordinary small cabin, probably belonging to one of the ship's officers. A card-table had been set up inside; and a man in a black suit sat behind it; but whether he was a policeman or an official of the shipping company I never found out. At this moment my eyes were held by further Dancer possessions spread on the table: some books, a writing case, the familiar Peregrine Potter wallet containing travel documents. A sense of foreboding began to fill me.

The man stood up rather awkwardly and gave a tiny bow and motioned me to sit down in a deck chair alongside the table. It put me absurdly low down in the world, so that my head was scarcely level with the edge of the table.

'You are not Mister Dancer,' said the official, half accusingly, half hopefully. His English was slow but not laborious. He pronounced 'Dancer' with a flat 'a'.

I shook my head. 'I was looking for him — you understand? Looking for him. Do you know where he is?'

'Yes, yes, in a moment. But first please give me your name.'

'Panton.'

'Aaaaah.' The official exhaled extravagantly. I saw that he had a duplicate of the cabin list in front of him. My name was ringed in red. 'You are his friend, perhaps?'

'Not exactly. I'm from the agency — the bureau, you know —' I pointed to the Peregrine Potter wallet. 'The cabin was booked in my name before it was known for certain if Mr Dancer would require it.' It seemed less complicated to put it that way. 'I happened to join this ship at Bodø so I thought I'd see if he was comfortable…'

The official contemplated the ringed name, and then picked up the wallet and put it down again and finally said. 'Well, we do not know what has become of your Dancer. He is not here any more.'

I stared at him. 'You mean he got left behind somewhere?' I'd been dreading some really unsettling news.

'There has been no report of anyone left behind at any of the ports of call during the night. But then we were asking about a Mister Panton, not a Dancer.' He looked at me reprovingly. 'We did not realize the change until we looked at these articles.'

'Yes, well, it was altered so late.'

'It must be said, however, that if an Englishman had been left behind anywhere we would surely have been told of it.'

'One would think so.'

'The passenger joined this ship at Trondheim.' I nodded agreement. 'He was aboard all yesterday, going ashore at some of the villages and ports on the route. It cannot be remembered if he had dinner last night. This morning his bed had not been slept in. The maid did not think too much at first, because during the Midnight Sun season tourists sometimes do not go to bed. But later she went back to the cabin and found everything the same there, so she told the ship's officers. They have told us in Bodø.'

'I see.'

'Last night there were several stops, the longest at Stamnes. It is possible he had some accident, but we would have normally heard something by this time. Or perhaps when the ship was between ports…' He left the sentence unfinished.

I was conscious of that massive, spurious detachment which is the first reaction to grave news. Something had happened to Dancer, something that was meant to happen to me. I was quite sure of it. But I could still inspect the proposition with objectivity, walk round it at leisure. A part of my mind got to work on practical details: should I tell Rogerson? What about a British consul? Perhaps I'd better change some more travellers' cheques, just in case. A drink would be nice.

The official was asking me about Dancer's itinerary. I told him. And where was I going? I explained briefly. He pursed his lips. 'It will not be easy to find you if we have any news.'

'I'm afraid not.'

'Or if we need any help from you.'

'I doubt if I could be of much help.'

'Perhaps if there were need for someone to identify…'

'Well, you see, I never met Mr Dancer. I only spoke to him on the telephone.' It was an instinctive lie. I hated getting involved. Besides, I had to go to Spitsbergen.

'I see. Anyway, we must hope he is safe and well somewhere, eh? Is he a man for the drink?'

'I'm not sure. I shouldn't have thought so.'

He rose to his feet again. I struggled up as best I could. He shook hands. 'We will contact you through the Spitsbergen ship company if we need. Goodbye.'

The willies really started to take over when I was on my own again. A queasy, irrational panic usurped the former detachment. A vision of Dancer's body floating soggily on some brown tide kept presenting itself, the face scoured and puffy, the nose and lips eroded. I had imaginary confrontations with Greeneyes, Rogerson, Potter. I was talking, explaining, denouncing, apologizing. Greeneyes was the villain and Donkey-jacket was his strong-arm man. I dreaded meeting him again and sidled round the ship shooting nervous glances behind me.

I began to feel hungry but didn't want to go back into the saloon. Twice I passed it and twice I saw Donkey-jacket humped over a beer. The third time he had gone and I tried to get a meal, but the service was worse than ever. I waited twenty minutes then beat it.

In the companionway outside I ran squarely into him. There was no escape. As I approached he opened the donkey-jacket and showed the neck of a bottle hidden underneath.

'I been looking for you. We drink some schnapps, heh?'

He took a gulp from the bottle, rubbed the mouth on his sleeve, and handed it to me. I took a cautious taste. It wasn't very nice. Not specially fiery, which I don't mind, but just rather sickly and over-flavoured with caraway seeds or something.

'Go on,' said Donkey-jacket. 'Have a real drink.'

'I've had enough, thanks. It was very nice.'

'That wasn't enough for a girl baby. Go on, drink.' He was scowling now. 'Aren't you a man or something?'

'I'd rather not. I haven't had anything to eat yet, you see.'

'Christ, what you want to eat for? The drink is better. You drink, heh?'

Suddenly I couldn't stand any more. Behind Donkey-jacket the companionway continued up to the top deck. I waited until it was clear, swung my grip up in front of me as a kind of guard, and shoved past him while his head was tilted drinking. As I went up the stairs two at a time I heard his voice, 'Heh you, heh.' I didn't look back, just circled the deck a few times, keeping close to people and watching the point of access like a hawk. After a while I found a vacant wicker chair in a nice protected corner giving me a good view of the deck. I grabbed it and settled down for a long vigil. The night stretched bleakly ahead and Midnight Sun or no Midnight Sun it was already beginning to get distinctly crepuscular.

Gradually the deck began to clear until only one large group remained. Someone was playing an accordion and a bunch of Norwegian matelots dressed in a variant of bell-bottoms were dancing and flirting with the girls they had met. Their leader was dark and handsome, almost Spanish in looks. His was the prettiest girl. She laughed as he steered her round the deck, a bottle of beer in his free hand. The sleeves of his tunic were rolled up, and he wore a red handkerchief carelessly round his neck. They were all so carefree and young. As long as they danced there I felt safe.

But to the west the Lofotens jutted up hugely, and the orb of the sun was getting lost behind them. I watched the time with agonizing concentration. At twenty minutes after midnight a fringe of cloud stifled the surviving rays and abruptly all was grey and cold. I was filled with fear that the dancers would disperse. For a while they did stop dancing, then one of them returned with a tray of coffee, and they stood drinking it. I looked so relieved that the prettiest girl smiled across at me. A few minutes later a thin shaft of orange light crept across the deck. The sun was rising again, and already I felt its warmth.

The dark sailor and the girl resumed their dancing. I dozed. At three in the morning we all went ashore at a fishing village where a vendor was selling frankfurters from a tankful on a barrow. I bought three. They were coarse and briny but welcome. The willies were over. Dancer had done some damn-fool trick like changing his mind yet again and jumping a south-bound boat back to Trondheim. Donkey-jacket was just a big yob whom I would never see again. Greeneyes was just a traveller, though I had to admit that his pinching the plane seat at Bodø rankled more than ever. I was going to Spitsbergen, soon I would see the amiable Randers, and when the saloon reopened I would have the biggest breakfast they could muster.

CHAPTER ELEVEN

Tromsø was the usual huddle of wharves, sheds, shiny aluminium oil tanks and dusty roads, if on a larger scale. After the cool of the sea it was fiercely hot, a steep hill behind the town seeming to trap the heat which poured down from the sun. On the quayside a stack of heavy black planks shimmered and danced. The *Bellsund*, someone said, was tied up at the other end of the harbour. I collected my things, pushed ashore and humped along the waterfront.

For a vessel plying within six hundred miles of the North Pole she wasn't very big. Nor was she very beautiful. A thin coil of smoke oozed from the single funnel. Ropes and boxes littered the deck. No one was in sight. I sneaked up the gangplank and stood uncertainly on a little covered deck amidships. I tried a tentative hullo. No reply.

There was a pile of luggage near me. I studied it for some clue as to fellow passengers. A set of expensive tan hide was prominent, labelled with Statler Hotel and airline labels. A rifle case was marked 'Westchester Country Club'. A blue kitbag looked to be of humbler origin, and two enormous rucksacks were clearly accustomed to second-class travel.

Further along were more rucksacks and bags, some recognizably War Department in pattern. I added my grip and decided to have a look at the town instead. There was still three hours to sailing time.

The Grand Hotel was a short toil uphill from the quay. Before I was half-way there I was sweating and my face and arms smarted from the long day in the unfiltered Scandinavian sun. Inside the foyer it was cool and almost luxurious. And sitting in an armchair, improbably reading an old *Punch*, was Greeneyes. On the impulse I went up to him, not sure what I would say. I found myself shouting.

'What do you mean by taking my seat on the plane? What's the big idea, mister?' God knows where the vocabulary came from. I was trembling with rage that came welling up, genuinely enough, I suppose, from some unsuspected reservoir. I could feel my chin quivering and — too late — my cheeks beginning to burn.

Greeneyes goggled. You could hardly blame him. '*Nicht Verstehen*.' He hunted round the foyer for possible help. Then for a moment we faced each other helplessly. The foolishness of my position overwhelmed me. I opened my mouth to say something, shut it again, turned on my heel. The girl behind the reception desk stared, a question trembling on her parted lips. I gave a wild sort of gesture to imply 'I'm all right, really,' and flapped out of the hotel.

In the rough dusty-red street I kicked myself for being such a nut and gazed fiercely into a shop window full of rather nice silver. There was a little brooch in the shape of a butterfly that would have pleased Jane. What to do now? After such a ridiculous scene it was hardly possible to go back into the hotel. Then I heard a familiar voice.

'Ah, so! The Colin!'

'Randers,' I said delightedly. It was marvellous to see someone I knew. 'How are you? Where've you been? Let's have a drink.'

'One minute, one minute. First tell me how you are. You are well?' He was shaking my hand and smiling but not the comical up-at-the-corners smile I remembered. He seemed thinner, older, more guarded.

'I'm fine.' I'd forgotten the absurd row already. 'But I'm starving. Can we get a meal before the boat sails?'

'Why, we will get dinner aboard.'

'I don't know if I can wait. I was on the lousy coastal steamer and I don't seem to have had anything except cheese and beer for three weeks.'

'There is the hotel restauration,' said Randers doubtfully. I'd forgotten the curious monochromatic quality he had, a sort of trick of melting into one colour scheme. Brown. Face, eyes, hair, suit, shirt, shoes, even the big Continental bow ties, were all brown.

'Um,' I said. I didn't really want to go back through the foyer.

'We go this way.' He led me past the main entrance to a side door up a few steps. I spotted a washroom and excused myself for a quick splash under the tap and a tidy up. With my hair combed, my tie tightened, I didn't look too wild.

Randers was at a table by the window.

'I think I'll start with a seal,' I said. Randers gave a perfunctory smile. I thought that would have gone down well with him. Obviously he wasn't his usual self.

'It is too early for dinner, they say. You can have an omelette if you like or cold dishes.'

I settled for a mushroom omelette. Randers consented to a beer but said he wouldn't eat. Something seemed to be on his mind.

'I had a look at the boat,' I babbled. 'Not very impressive.'

'Nao.'

'Miss Penywern. How is Miss Penywern?'

A flicker of interest. 'She is on holiday with her friend, Miss Robinson. They are in Bodmin in the Duchy of Cornwall.'

'How lovely for them.' I buttered a piece of dark brown bread.

'Col?' The time for blurting out had come.

'Yes?'

'Col, why did you trouble the Dr Bland? He is very upset.'

'*Who*? How do you mean?' But, of course, it was obvious.

'The person in the hotel foyer you cried at.'

'Oh, *that*.' So my instinct about the man had been well founded. 'It was rather silly. I was all steamed up. I had an idea he'd kept me off the plane at Bodø. I had no idea it was Bland. Anyway, you've never mentioned any Bland to me...'

'Why should he want to keep you off the plane? He had never seen you before, unless it was on the fly from Oslo.'

'You still haven't told me who he is.'

'He is Dr Bland, one of our associates in the sheem.'

'Scheme,' I said mechanically.

'You haven't helped me, you knao, by doing that thing.'

'All right, I'm sorry.'

'What became of you, dear fellow, to behave so? It is really most embarrassing. The Dr Bland is troubled.'

'I said I'm sorry.'

'He has been one of those who had no wish to share the sheem with English tourists. I have had great difficulty in conquering his objections.'

I was beginning to be glad that I had troubled the Dr Bland. 'But have you conquered them?'

'Why do you say that?'

'Well, honestly, it seems obvious to me that we're being squeezed out.'

'That is not true, Col.' He gazed with reproachful eyes. 'Mr Potter has been losing interest for some time now. I have had to make the lead, eh?'

This was partly true. I privately conceded. I said, 'What about Bland? He went over both our heads to Edinburgh.'

Randers shrugged. 'He has negotiated directly with Ferguson, Roberts and Holburn S.S.C., because there was need for haste. In any case, it was not concerning you to buy the land. It was only for travel possibilities you were interested.'

I swallowed a mouthful of bread. 'Yeah. And look what's happening there! First it was going to be just a guesthouse, then a holiday camp across the fjord, and now some sort of assault course for Deutscher pioneers who want to live the life rigorous. Where are our lecturers in modern languages supposed to fit in?'

Randers was puzzled. 'I don't knao what you mean by lecturers in modern languages. I haven't been told of any lecturers in modern languages.'

'A figure of speech. People. Our clients. They like the holiday different maybe but not necessarily the life rigorous.'

'Now, Col, please understand.' He leaned forward earnestly. 'It is not my designing. I am only the agent. I admit the sheem has changed much. But I think it is more *practical* now. Think, Col, would there ever have been enough custom from luxury people? Perhaps twenty or thirty a year? But we knao there is always demand from young people.'

The omelette was arriving, with a clatter of plates and cutlery.

'Students,' said Randers. 'Young mechanics and builders. All those. And of course we will be helped in the cost. Many big businesses are interested to help. You knao that?'

'Okay. We'll see.' I rested on that for the time being and let myself brighten. I drank some beer. I said, 'Tell me about the *Bellsund*. She looks a bit of a tub, I must say.'

Randers relaxed visibly. The corners of his mouth turned up parallel to the ends of his bow tie.

'She is not the *Queen Mary* or *Elizabeth*,' he beamed, 'that is certain. But she was built for Nordmeer — how do you say that? North Sea, nao. Polar Sea?'

'Arctic Ocean, I suppose.'

'Arctic Ocean, of course. So she is very strong, very seaworthy. The sea is very rough, you knao. I am dreadful of it — nao, I am *dreading* it. I am so seasick.'

'I'm usually all right. You should eat now, then. Make the most of dry land.'

'That is not necessary. The first part of the voyage is through quite sheltered waters.'

'Are there many other passengers?'

'Oh yes, quite a crowd of us. There are many of your compatriots — students from Oxford or Cambridge University, I forget which. They are going on an expedition, you knao. They are travelling steerage. There must be twenty of them at least, and they have a small boat they were trying out in the harbour yesterday. The Dr Bland thought they looked fine young men.'

'Who else?'

'There are some officials returning to the islands, I am told, and a nurse to the hospital at Longyear A small party of mountain-climbers, I think they are French. You will see them all. Oh yes, and there is a very funny American couple. You will laugh when I tell you.'

I doubted so, but I smiled politely in readiness.

'They are going hunting up in Svalbard. You can hire a boat and crew. But do you knao what they have done? They have brought a cinema cameraman with them to film all they do!'

'Heavens!' I didn't have the heart to spoil Randers's glee by letting on I'd already seen them.

'Yes, truly. Today I have seen them shooting the arrival of the Ju-plane from Tromsø. Factually, they have come yesterday, but, of course, the cameraman was with them. So today they pretended it all over again, even climbing aboard the plane so they could be photographed coming off it.'

'Goodness.'

'The wife is an awful woman. She has red hair and a loud voice. We have named her "The Terrible Woman".'

'I think I saw her on the plane from Oslo.'

'Of course! You were on the same one as Dr Bland. He also saw them.'

A question occurred to me. Why had Bland come through Norway at all? Randers had come via Stockholm, which was the obvious way from Berlin. Surely it would have been logical for them to travel together? But for the time being I said nothing about it.

Aboard the *Bellsund* again all was activity. The Oxford or Cambridge explorers were much in evidence, loud and hearty. I didn't recognize anyone else. Maybe the American couple had already staged their embarkation.

Randers had arranged for us to share a cabin. It was quite pleasant in a practical, white-painted way. I found a shower along the passageway and had a warm salty spray and put on a clean shirt and lay on my bunk with the bird book, ignoring the dinner gong which bonged within minutes of casting-off. I'd eaten enough.

The Arctic Tern, I learned, could be distinguished from the common tern by the accent on the *second* syllable in the distress cry *kee-ar*. I tried it out. *Kee*-ar. Kee-*ar*. If I cricked my neck I could see green islets sliding past the porthole.

CHAPTER TWELVE

I awoke to the awareness of considerable motion. Obviously we were at sea. The bunk was tilting rhythmically from right to left and back to right again. I found myself stiffening to resist it. Uh-huh. The thing to do was not to fight. Just relax. Go with it. I slithered against the side. Was that the suspicion of a headache? Of sickness? I sat up. Through the porthole, sea and sky were uniformly grey. Flying spray sped by. A low-beating seabird skimmed into view, then rose and vanished again. I lay back and dozed rather queasily until it was time to get up. Randers slept on in the other bunk.

At breakfast there were many defections, according to Randers. He didn't look too good himself, but doggedly spooned into a boiled egg. The saloon was not a bad little place, on a level with the upper deck and fairly bright. There were three tables, each capable of holding about eight people, but now with more empty places than full. A big silent girl who turned out to be the nurse going to the hospital at Longyear sat to my left. At the next table, in a sunburnt huddle, was the party of French climbers, a little apart from them sat a thin sharp man with a death's-head face and pink eyes. I caught the cadence of his voice and knew him for a Swede. He was a tourist, I discovered later, the only genuine round-tripper in the first-class unless you counted in Randers and me. Just now he was talking sporadically to the little bearded man I remembered as the Americans' cameraman. Of the Americans themselves there was no sign.

Nor was Dr Bland in evidence. 'He is sitting at the Captain's table,' said Randers, indicating the furthest one from us. 'Perhaps he has had his breakfast already.'

'Not with you, then.'

'Nao. We are only business associates in the sheem. He stays to himself a lot, you knao. He has made this voyage before, so he is friend of the captain.'

The last sentence seemed to come out with difficulty. 'Are you all right?' I asked. Randers looked worse. He had taken a mouthful of coffee but seemed reluctant to swallow it. A dribble was escaping from the corner of his mouth, and on his upper lip gleamed a faint perspiration. Abstractedly he pushed the boiled egg away. As the ship rolled it trundled back towards him. He got up and hastened out.

I felt a certain sharpness in my own salivary glands, but forced myself to finish the bread and jam I was eating and drink another cup of coffee, which was very good, before going on deck for a blow. The wind was cold. The sea was grey and heaving, the sky opaque. Gone were the green islets and sparkling waters of the previous evening. Overnight we were out of Europe and into the Arctic.

With occasional side-stepping and grabbing of rails, perambulation wasn't too difficult. There was really only one deck, except for a tiny surround to the saloon and a raised open deck aft. I worked my way round to the stern from where trailed — literally — the ship's log, a cable which revolved as it was rowed through the water, clocking up the miles on a massive brass dial.

'Primitive,' said a voice, 'but nobody has thought of anything very much better.'

I turned. It was Greeneyes, or Dr Bland as I'd better call him from now on.

'Oh, hallo.'

There was a moment of appraisal.

'It says 130 already,' I added, for something to say. 'Would that be miles or kilometres?'

'Nautical miles, I think. On the sea it is customary.' His English was slow but correct, with a hint of Americanization.

I said, 'It seems I owe you an apology. About yesterday, I mean. It was silly of me.'

'It is already forgotten. Shall we take a walk around the deck?'

We took one turn, then another. Conversationally it wasn't a great success. Though Bland always seemed a strong and erect figure he was short when you stood close to him. I was taller by a head, which always makes upright relations difficult. You stoop, the other one looks up. I felt long and awkward, like a farm-boy. Also my nose was running, and I had no handkerchief.

'We must have a long talk about our plans in Svalbard,' Bland was saying.

I sniffed. 'Yes, of course.'

'Perhaps it would be more pleasant inside. We could meet in the saloon and perhaps have something to drink.'

'Good idea.' I warmed towards him about one degree Fahrenheit.

'Mr Randers should be present also.'

'Indeed. Unfortunately he's not quite himself at the moment. He's terribly seasick.'

'I had heard so. We must wait until he is better.'

But Randers didn't pick up all day. He lay in his bunk sleeping uneasily, a basin by his side.

CHAPTER THIRTEEN

It was about mid-morning when I rumbled the fact that there was some talent aboard. Two girls, to be exact. They were on deck when I went for another traipse round. A bunch of the university explorers were also taking the air. Loud young voices, loud young laughter caught by the wind, hands thrust into the pockets of corduroy trousers. An awareness of the opposite sex across the deck, but no direct acknowledgment of it. The girls stood apart, looking out over the tossing waves, pretending to be oblivious. They wore climbing jackets, or anoraks, with the hoods up, and dark blue slacks. Until they turned, it was hard to tell much more about them except that one was shorter and slighter than the other.

They turned as I was lurching behind them — for the boat was still rolling about — a second time. I smiled. They smiled back. The taller one was dark, with rather coarse good looks. Her smile held a hint of metal and her eye, as they used to say, was bold. The littler one was shy — her eyes dropped after a fraction of a second. But they were eyes of shining liquid brownness, like Pears Soap, and her face was the kind of little heart-shaped, tilted face of childish candour that had always been my special weakness. I passed on, mumbling a 'good-day' or something which was snatched away by the wind. By the time I could decently look back they'd gone.

At lunch I met the radio officer, who had a side responsibility to look after the social welfare of the passengers. He was a nice enough, nondescript little man in shabby blue uniform and brown shoes. Well, why not? He tried to sell me a subscription to some Arctic travellers' society. I couldn't quite see the benefits of it, and anyway I had something else on my mind. I asked him.

'The two girls,' he said, 'they are Finnish. From Finland. They are in the second class. We hope they will be all right among all the expedition boys, eh?' He didn't make a joke of it, but just gave the sentence a kind of worldly tiredness.

'Quite.'

'Of course, they have their own cabin. There is also a little day saloon for second-class women where they can sit.'

'What brings them on this journey? From Finland I should have thought you'd want to get somewhere hot, quick.'

'They are interested, I guess.' Obviously he didn't care much. 'You should ask your seasick friend Mr Randers. He has sent many people on this voyage. You in the travel business also?'

'Not really.' It turned out to be a lucky evasion.

'Travel is okay. I used to be in the Olsen Line. America, South America, Singapore, Batavia, everywhere. Another time I was in the weather service and stayed in one place six months, maybe a year. Jan Mayen, you know, out in the Atlantic. Then Cap Linné on Svalbard. Now I've a house in Tromsø and two kids at school and I'm home every eight days in winter and every twelve in summer, like anyone else.' He shrugged. 'It's okay, too.'

The Americans didn't put in an appearance until dinner. They sat at the captain's table. The man was the one who had been sick, I guessed. Or the sicker of the two. He looked pale and incredibly frail. Without a hat his head was bare and bony and it hung forward from his shoulders as if he were ducking to get through a low doorway. The woman was more fantastic than ever. She wore a suede jacket studded with brass nails over a black dress that had the sort of simplicity that costs a lot of francs. Her legs were still thrust into Texan boots — white ones. The great upswept coif of red hair glowed anilinely. Her strident voice and laugh punctuated the meal.

I watched Bland curiously to see his reactions, but he kept his head down, eating methodically and talking to his neighbour. Only the Swedish tourist at the far table stared continuously at the couple, his little pink eyes alight with distaste.

'I must say they're a pair of weirdies,' I said.

The radio officer remained professionally unimpressed. 'You should have seen some we carried on the South America run. They're all right.'

'What's the name?'

'Rennick. Something like that. From New York. They must be rich. They're going on a hunting trip on the *Harriet*. That's a private ketch you can hire in Svalbard. The charter costs a thousand kroner a day. What's that — fifty pounds?'

I nodded and looked across the little saloon with new respect. Fifty quid a day, eh? I half wished to make a closer acquaintance with them but as soon as they'd had a few sips of soup and pecked at the rather awful cutlets they left the saloon again. The captain and his first mate rose and bowed awkwardly as the old man shuffled to the door. He was leaning heavily on his wife's arm and I saw the look on her face as she steered him through the door, a sort of tenderness for one person and defiance for everyone else.

'I think she used to be his nurse,' said the radio officer, perceptively.

'Oh dear, Col, I feel so terrible,' said Randers faintly. I had to admit he looked pretty ghastly. He'd asked me to fetch him a cup of tea from the saloon, with a little milk but no sugar.

'You can get drugs against this sort of thing nowadays,' I said.

'They will not help me.' He closed his eyes. 'In my briefcase, the good *traubenzucker*. Can you find a piece, please, and put it in the tea?'

The briefcase was the sort every German carries, if only to hold his liverwurst sandwiches. I opened the flap and hunted inside. There was a magazine, some papers, a long-playing record in a gay sleeve and down at the bottom some wrapped glucose tablets. The oddity of the odd item didn't strike me at first.

Randers propped himself up on one elbow and sipped the tea.

'Randers,' I said slyly. 'What was Dr Bland doing in Oslo? Why didn't you come together through Stockholm?'

'I don't knao. I think he had business there.' He gulped more tea.

'And Randers.' Something else had struck me now. 'Why are you taking a record to the Arctic?' I had another look. 'A record of Berlioz's *Symphonie Funèbre et Triomphale*, of all things?'

Randers pushed the cup at me and lay back. He groaned. He was feeling the nausea again. I repeated the question.

'It is for the Dr Bland. He asked me…' His voice trailed away, whether from illness or discretion I knew not. A moment later back came the tea, mostly over my trousers. That's what you get for being kind.

The radio officer was in a little office by the companionway, closed to passengers, that led up to the bridge. The door was open; on the impulse I stopped and poked my head inside. An operator in a stained reefer jacket was drinking a mug of coffee, earphones eased forward off his ears. The radio officer was copying on to a cable form something which had been scribbled out on a message pad. He wrote carefully, in block letters.

He looked up. 'Cable for Mr Rennick. It's his birthday. There's greetings and Happy Hunting from Arlene and Nelson, Caroline and Nelson Junior.'

I said, 'Do you pick up news broadcasts?'

'Most times.'

'Have you heard anything at all about an Englishman called Dancer? He went missing from the coastal steamer I was on.'

The operator shook his head before the radio officer could pass on the question. I filled in a few more details. They promised to let me know if they heard anything.

CHAPTER FOURTEEN

In the middle of the night we passed Bear Island, which was apparently always an event. I heard the commotion, pulled on some clothes, and went on deck. The light was the same greyish white it had been all day. The island loomed to port. Thousands of seabirds wheeled and swirled around the ship; and from the high cliffs came the murmur of millions more. Along the rails crew members and university explorers were casting lines into the sea and hauling them up again hooked into fat wriggling fish.

'Cod,' said the radio officer. 'If you are fortunate you just pull it out of the sea here. We have it for dinner tomorrow.'

The Americans had emerged, watching the scene and being filmed watching it by their tireless man. Old Rennick, huddled in a check lumber jacket, peered out from beneath a long-peaked ski-cap. He looked better. Mrs had donned a coat of white wool. The captain was by her side.

I looked for the girls and didn't spot them for a minute or two. They stood a little back, by the companionway that led to the after deck, and by them stood three — no, four — of the explorers. As I watched there was one of them proffering cigarettes. The taller girl took one, the smaller didn't. That was something, anyway. I strained my ears to catch what the braying public school voices were saying.

Just then there was a distraction.

'Jesus!' The exclamation rang out. It was Ma Rennick. A hovering gull had defecated oilily on the sleeve of her white coat. The captain whipped out a handkerchief. Everyone else stared in silence. The Rennick woman regarded the damage.

'Okay, so it means good luck!' she said finally. Then throwing back her head she bellowed with harsh loud laughter. It rolled away from the ship like cannon fire and moments later came echoing back from the island cliffs, until it was engulfed in the hubbub of alarmed seabirds.

They opened up the saloon for hot chocolate, or alcohol if you wanted, which was nice. This time I managed my meeting with old Rennick.

'What brings you on this trip, Mr Prontor?' he asked after we'd exchanged the usual pleasantries.

It was a question I hadn't really settled for myself yet. The mission for Potter sounded awfully tame, the mission for Rogerson too tenuous. I improvised. 'I'm a writer, actually. In the films. I had an idea for a scenario set up here — you know, *politische* outdoor adventure. Icebergs and Russians, all in Cinemascope!' Now I thought of it, it wasn't a bad idea.

Rennick weighed up what I had said. The old watery eyes blinked once. 'I see. I see. Kind of espionage thriller in a Polar setting. Could make a good movie. The only thing is that Fox made one up in the Aleutians with icebergs and Russians and Cinemascope. And it didn't do too well.'

'You seem to know all about it.' I felt a bit cut down.

'I work in a bank,' said Rennick, 'lending money to make movies. That's my job.'

CHAPTER FIFTEEN

Next day brought the first glimpse of Spitsbergen. As I went tramping round the deck for the umpteenth time people were standing on the starboard bow, pointing. The Swedish tourist had produced a pair of binoculars. Far away in the distance tiny white conical peaks pricked up through the mist. They looked remote and identical and perfect. The wind carried the faint smell of snow.

'South Cape,' said the radio officer. The explorers stared respectfully.

One of them said, 'There was a party from Oxford there a couple of years ago. Gregg knows about it. I think he nearly went or something.'

'Does anyone live there?' The explorers looked at me haughtily. It wasn't the thing to ask.

'A few trappers,' said the radio officer. 'And there is the wireless station.'

Sunlight was beginning to filter through the cloud. It caught the crest of the waves, making them sparkle. To the east a ray touched one of the tiny peaks and it winked like a jewel. I identified two guillemots alongside the ship, beating their little pointed wings, briefly planing, beating again.

'Are you a journalist?' One of the explorers was trying to be friendly, anyway. He was a nice-looking boy with fair hair and an embryo beard.

I said, 'No. It's rather sad for you but I'm just a tourist.'

'Why should that be sad?'

'I thought it would be a bit defeating for an explorer to find himself on the same boat as a tourist.'

'Good lord, no. I don't go in for that line. Some of the chaps do, though. They probably wouldn't be too pleased. If anything, I'm jealous.'

I gave him a cigarette.

'I mean, I'd rather be a tourist like you, really. Comfort. I'm greatly in favour of comfort.'

'It is rather nice,' I agreed.

He jerked his head in the direction of the others. 'All *they* talk about is ice-falls and pemmican and day's marches and pulling teeth out without an anaesthetic. God, I don't know how I'm going to stick six weeks of them. It's like being back in the O.T.C.'

'Where are you going exactly?'

'Somewhere called Wide-fjord or something like that. Miles from bloody anywhere. The Governor's boat is going to take us from Longyear. Then some of the chaps are going to cross an ice-cap right over to the east coast. Not me, though. I'm not the right sort. Strictly a base-wallah.'

'What's the expedition going to do?'

'Usual thing: test a few bits of equipment for firms. Do some surveys. We've got a lot of stone-chippers in the party. And develop our characters, of course.'

'I know,' I said sympathetically. 'They tried to do that to me in the army. String vests and humping things over mountains in the Highlands. Still, you'll probably have a lot of fun.'

'I hope so.' He didn't sound very optimistic.

I said, 'You must come and have a drink in the posh part.'

'That would be marvellous.'

'I think I've got to have a sort of business session before lunch. If so, this evening perhaps?'

'Fine.'

'Where do I find you?'

'Around here. Or down the fetid hold.'

'Is it rough?'

'No, I'm only kidding. It's jolly nice, really. Proper bunks. Very clean. Those eiderdown things. Rather a lot of bods in one room, that's all.'

I said guardedly, 'There are a couple of chicks billeted with you, aren't there? I've seen them around.'

'Not really with us. They've got their own cabin somewhere. All the company we've got is a dead bod. Charming.'

'What?'

'Honestly. We found him last night. In the baggage hold, and the baggage hold leads off our hold. A bloody great white coffin.'

I stared at him blankly, revolving the intelligence. 'Can you show me?'

'I don't see why not. It's mostly our stuff that's down there.'

'Now?'

He thought. 'It's as good a time as any. A few of the chaps are bound to be around, but that won't matter. As long as the Leader's not there. He's a bit fussy.'

The explorer led the way forward and down a steep companionway.

'Who's the Leader?' I asked, still speculating privately about the white coffin.

'Oh, he's an efficient sort of sod. Third year Mechanical Sciences. Been here twice before. We're all Cambridge except four from Exeter. There's a couple of Sapper officers but I think they were Cambridge originally.'

We passed through a narrow room with a narrow table and benches down the centre, and into a wedge-shaped cabin beyond. Two tiers of bunks lined the walls, one or two occupied by reading explorers. At the far end was a small iron door held by two bolts.

'What do I call you?' I whispered.

'Peter.'

'My name's Panton. Colin Panton.'

Peter slid back the bolts. 'We tried it for luck,' he explained. 'It opened.'

We squeezed through the aperture into darkness. A wafer of light from the edge of the hatch-cover above showed a dark mass of piled boxes and bundled tents. Peter groped behind the door and turned a switch. Electric light jumped on. The hold was an even narrower wedge, almost triangular. We were evidently in the very bows of the ship.

Peter whispered, 'There it is,' but I'd already seen.

I was positive it was the one that had been en route at Bodø. Shaped the age-old coffin shape but somehow different in execution. I went nearer and fingered the side. It was cold and metallic. The colour was silvery rather than white.

'Steel?' I asked.

'Feels more like aluminium to me. We could tell by lifting.'

'No thanks.'

There was a handle at each end, and some code letters stencilled on the side, and a stencilled cross. Above these marks someone had written something more amateurishly, in clumsy black paint that had run down in dribbles.

'It's Spanish,' said Peter. 'Something about Handle with Reverence.'

'No destination mentioned?'

'Can't see one.'

I had another long look to make sure. There could be no mistake. It was the same coffin, all right.

'The rest is mostly ours,' said Peter. There were bundles and cases and kitbags, some big carboys in wicker baskets, and lots of wooden crates. 'Full of rations and jars of Bovril and rolls of brown bog paper. There are sledges somewhere. And we've got a boat up on deck.'

'Yes, I saw it.'

'The Leader bought it in Tromsø. I hope he wasn't rooked.'

We went back on deck, carefully putting out the light and closing the bolts.

CHAPTER SIXTEEN

Rander s was much improved. He had made a cautious breakfast in the cabin, and felt well enough to get up. At elevenses-time (the *Bellsund's* tireless meal schedule also included afternoon tea) he was drinking coffee and cream in the saloon. He'd seen the Dr Bland and we would have our meeting before lunch if that was all right.

'Sure,' I said. *It was the same coffin, without doubt.*

'Ah, Col, I did feel so horrible! I am so grateful for your kindness.'

'I wasn't any help at all.' *Where was it going?*

'When I write to Miss Penywern I will tell her how you looked after me.'

'Nuts.' *And what was Bland's interest?*

'Col, do you remember the time in Berlin you were so sick after drinking too much sekt?'

'Sorry, what was that?'

'The time you were sick after drinking too much champagne?'

'Oh yes, of course.'

I found the radio officer in the little office below the bridge.

'On second thoughts,' I said, 'I'd like to join that Arctic Club of yours.'

'Ah good. You like the Arctic now, I think.'

'It's acquiring a certain charm.'

'Ja, everyone feels that, I guess.' Inconsistently he added, 'Me, I see it all enough. I'd be okay home in Tromsø with the woman and the children.' He rummaged round in his desk and found a book of coupons like raffle tickets.

'Your name. Full name.'

'Colin Panton.' I thought I could skip the Robin. I never liked it.

'Yes, but what do you do?'

Luckily I hadn't committed myself to the travel business. 'Journalist.'

'Ah, you're one of them. You write for the newspapers?'

'Mm.'

'Which one?'

'*The Times*,' I lied. It didn't make much impression. Perhaps I should have said the *Mail* or *Express* or *Paris-Match*.

The radio officer wrote out the coupon in big block letters: JOURNALISTE COLIN PANTON. 'Address?'

I gave Printing House Square, to be consistent if nothing else. I said, 'I'm really on holiday. But I thought I might write something about Spitsbergen now I'm here.'

'Ah yes, you should do that.'

'But it won't be any good just doing the usual what-I-saw business. I'll need to stunt it up a bit.'

'Please?'

'*The Times* is a very popular newspaper, you understand. For shop-girls and people like that. I'm afraid our readers wouldn't be interested in snow and ice and coal production and so on.'

The radio officer nodded knowledgeably.

'What my editor likes is a nice off-beat story full of human interest. Supposing some rich Oslo girl had Given Up Everything and run away to Spitsbergen to marry a miner. And her father rushed up on the next boat to fetch her back. Something like that…'

I regarded the radio officer brightly. He frowned a profound frown and scratched his head. 'I haven't heard of just that story,' he declared finally. 'There was a miner once who had two women and two lots of children I heard of, that's all. One in Lillehammer and one in some other place. They found out when he put the wrong letter in the wrong envelope.'

I stretched my face into a wide smile. 'Really?' I said encouragingly. 'Fancy. That's the sort of thing. But not quite enough human interest for *The Times*. I'll tell you what. How about that coffin? The one down below?'

'Ah, the coffin. It's some man who worked in Svalbard once, wants to be buried there. That's all.'

'That could be a good story for me. Marvellous. The man who loved the Arctic! Perhaps he worked here as a young man, fell in love with the place. He went away to make his fortune in a far-away country but he never forgot those nights under the Pole Star! When the end of his life was approaching he made a last request: that his body should return to the land his spirit had always yearned for!'

'Sure,' said the radio officer. 'That is a good one. Sure.' He sat back satisfied.

'But I need to find out a bit more about him,' I said gently. 'His name, for example. Where he comes from. Do you think you can help?'

The radio officer filled his pipe. I waited. Then he grunted and pushed himself to his feet. I followed him out of the office past a couple of doors and through a third. The first mate lay on his bunk reading a book. The cabin smelled of feet. He had a heavy, soapy face with dyspeptic lines weighing down the corners of his mouth.

He listened as the radio officer spoke briefly in Norwegian, then asked one question. The radio officer replied. The first mate swung his legs off the bunk and reached into a little bureau. He handed me a brown envelope with the end slit open. While the two officers conversed fitfully I examined the contents. There were two letters in Norwegian; a sealed envelope addressed to the Sysselman, which I knew meant the Governor of Spitsbergen; and some forms, one in Spanish. The nationality of the dead man was American. Place of Death: Exaltacion, in Bolivia. He had been flown to Rio by Aerovias, onwards by S.A.S. His name headed every letter and jumped in block capitals from every form. He was Williams, Harry Williams, Arctic Pioneer.

The radio officer was translating, 'It says that this is the dead man advised in a previous message. He is to go to Ny Alesund for burial. He was not a Catholic. The instructions for burial are in the letter to the Sysselman. That is all.'

CHAPTER SEVENTEEN

In the saloon, the tables were already laid for the midday meal, though it would be another hour before the gong went. Randers had been on deck for some fresh air and looked still further recovered. He had put on a pair of those uncertain Continental plus-fours, very baggy trousers zooming down to be nipped in to the leg at the last moment. With his bow tie, and a pair of dark glasses he had donned to indicate frailty, he looked more than ever a parody of a matinée idol from a prewar German movie.

Bland sat straight and composed at his side. A notebook and fountain pen were neatly arranged before him. He said 'First let us order something to drink. What would you prefer, Mr Panton?'

I said I thought I'd have some aquavit. I hadn't had any so far this trip.

'Randers?'

Randers looked uncomfortable. 'Oh, a beer, I think.'

'Is that wise so soon after illness?'

'Perhaps a little brandy, then, with water. That is good for the stomach. Yes, a brandy.' He was defiant now and rather pleased with himself.

Bland shrugged. 'As you wish. If you'll excuse me, Mr Panton, I will take a soft drink only. I rarely touch alcohol.' He ordered the drinks from the steward, an Apfelsaft for himself.

There was a pause while we waited.

I said to Bland, 'I believe you have been to Spitsbergen before?'

'Several times. You also?'

I shook my head.

'It is a fascinating country. Wild and beautiful and like no other country I have seen.' But there was no light of enthusiasm in the hard eyes behind the green glasses. I was struck by the bloom of his appearance. No other word will quite do. His face was unlined, the skin smooth and tanned. The fringe of hair that was left him held not a trace of grey. His hands were perfectly maintained and perfectly *still*. I never saw them make an unpremeditated movement. Like Rogerson he might have been anything between fifty and sixty-five. Unlike Rogerson he looked only fifty.

The drinks arrived. The aquavit came in the bottle. The steward poured out a tall thin glassful and thoughtfully left the rest.

'Skal,' said Randers.

'Skal,' we agreed.

The aquavit was cold and sharp. I liked it. Bland sipped his apple juice and set the glass down.

'Mr Panton,' he said levelly, 'you have perhaps been misled by our Spartapol scheme. I think it is my fault.' But he gave Randers a critical glance.

I waited.

'What we have in mind, Mr Panton, is a place where our young people — and those from other countries — can live hard for a little while. Climb mountains and explore and fend for themselves.' He paused fractionally for effect. 'In the second class there are many young Englishmen from the university. They are going to do exactly what we would like to give our young people.'

'They're a scientific expedition,' I protested. 'They've got some job to do. A geological survey.'

'It is a small part, I think.'

'They go for fun,' put in Randers.

'They go,' said Bland, 'because they are young, adventurous and healthy and they have had enough of the towns and petrol fumes. It is a good thing. But they are at the university. They have plenty of time — the long break in the summer. They have plenty of money…'

'Not necessarily. They travel very cheaply. And they get grants and equipment and things from industry.'

'Quite so, quite so. We shall hope to have the same help. But you will agree that most of them are young men of leisure and privilege. This long vacation of theirs is a privilege in itself. We are wanting to help young people who have not such good opportunities. Apprentices, technical pupils, students at the university who have little money…'

Though his English was excellent, I noticed he always accented the second syllable of 'student', as if to retain the clipped, disciplined ring of the German word.

'You must agree it is a fine inspiration, Colin,' said Randers. He refilled my glass.

'With only four weeks off from their work,' Bland went on, 'we hope to give them at least a fortnight at Spartapol — more as soon as we can arrange some form of air transport.' He looked at me pointedly. 'That is what I was examining in Oslo.'

I held his gaze.

'Unfortunately such a scheme would not fit in with your needs, Mr Panton. I think it would be like trying to mix soldiers and civilians, or first-class and tourist-class passengers.'

'Well, not exactly…'

'To be candid, Mr Panton, I am not sure that your needs can be met on Svalbard at all. You will excuse me speaking bluntly like this, but I wish to save you wasting more money. The idea of a hotel there goes back a long time. There have been two attempts which failed.'

'I know,' I said. 'I heard about them from Rogerson.'

'Before the First World War Svalbard was very popular with tourists, you know. Especially tourists from my country. Quite large ships used to go there on North Pole Cruises, as they called them. But even then the hotels could not thrive. I do not think they could thrive now.'

I looked at Randers.

'I am afraid the Doctor is correct, Col. The old sheem was unrealistic.'

'Would you still be willing to join with Potter in a modified scheme?'

Randers hesitated. 'For myself? I don't knao…'

I drained the second glass of aquavit.

Bland said, 'If you are still resolved to have a hotel I can perhaps help you. I would suggest something in Ny Alesund, where the North Pole Hotel was formerly.'

'Where would we find the money? Peregrine Potter is a small agency.'

'I wasn't thinking of anything deluxe. There is a building in Ny Alesund which I believe you could have. It is only timber, but it is very much like the old North Pole Hotel.'

'How do you know it would be available?'

'Because we made inquiries ourselves at one time. I have stayed in it. I expect to stay in it this time. It is not very grand. It was used as a miner's hostel. Now the mines are hardly working it is not often occupied. It would need some work on it. But it is sound.'

I said, 'Thank you. It was nice of you to think of us.' Actually, of course, it was just about the least they could have done. But I was feeling mellowed and even a bit stupid. The aquavit was strong, on top of the sea air.

Bland filled my glass a third time. 'In return,' he said thoughtfully, 'you may be able to do something for me.'

'How?'

'You know Mr Rogerson, I believe. He has much influence. You could put in a good word for us.'

'I doubt if that will be necessary,' I said. 'He's pretty pro-you already.'

Bland permitted himself the merest inclination of his head in acknowledgment. Randers beamed. He did so like people to get on together. I promised myself to be nasty to him later. The saloon was beginning to fill up for lunch. I rose.

I ate more than usual of the cold table and had a couple of beers with it. Moreover Randers insisted on buying me a brandy afterwards. As I collapsed into an easy chair to doze it all off I felt replete and rather amorous. I wondered how to get to know the Finnish girls. The introduction was to come from an unexpected source.

CHAPTER EIGHTEEN

All afternoon we continued to steam up the coast of West Spitsbergen. The conical mountains lined the horizon. As visibility improved they stood out more sharply against an eggshell-blue sky, tiny and yet near-seeming. Sometimes the coastline was broken by gleaming blue-white cliffs, the mouths of glaciers. One stretched for miles. 'The source of many of the icebergs which infest the North Atlantic in winter,' said a little booklet they'd dished us out with, gratis. There was no sign of life except for the ever-present birds. I identified storm-gulls, fulmars, and what might have been a little auk.

Up on the after-deck the Rennicks' cameraman was posing them for a linking shot. The old man stood with outstretched arm. She nodded her head mutely. Then the other way about: she pointing, he nodding.

'Such people,' said Randers crossly. He had crammed a little knitted hat on his head. The bobble bobbed vigorously as he spoke.

Looking beyond him I spotted the Finnish girls at last. To my astonishment they were following Bland, obviously in tow. The bigger one smiled at me. The three of them approached.

'The Americans continue their film,' said Randers. 'They are acting now the first sight of the promised land.'

Bland ignored him. He said, 'Mr Panton, there was something I forgot to ask you this morning. These young men from the university party — do you know any of them?'

'I've talked to one boy, that's all.' What on earth was coming next?

Bland said, 'I should very much like to meet him.' He stopped, in something as near to embarrassment as I ever saw him. 'He would perhaps help us.'

Randers stepped forward dutifully. 'Of course, the pictures. I have forgotten.' He explained. 'We wish to take some photographs for a prospectus we will make as soon as the sheem is approved. And the Dr Bland feels we should have some figures in the foreground to make them more interesting.'

I wanted to laugh. It was so unexpected and yet so weirdly predictable. I remembered the old boys' magazine cliché about Tuetonic thoroughness.

'We have no young people of our own in Svalbard yet,' said Bland. 'So we must "borrow" a pair. Miss Pori here, from Finland, has agreed to help —' he indicated the little fair girl — 'and now we need a boy.'

'My friends tell me I don't look a day over twenty-nine,' I said. 'Won't I do?'

Randers chortled. 'We would have someone who does not look more than *nineteen*. I saw your friend this morning from the saloon. I think he would be excellent for our purpose.'

'Peter? I'll ask him.' But already the idea was beginning to disturb me.

The little Finnish girl had shed her anorak and wore a dark blue shirt with the sleeves rolled back from forearms gleaming smoothly in the sun. She was perched on the upturned keel of the explorers' boat stored on the extreme foredeck of the *Bellsund*. The cloth of her blue trousers was stretched tight over flanks which spread out from a tiny waist in that precision of line which is the perfect complement to the curves that follow. In other words, she had a nice little seat. Also, her hair shone short and straight like cornsilk and her laugh, when it rang out, was like a silver bell. She looked seventeen and she made me feel something which I hadn't felt since I was seventeen — a kind of immediate, instinctive jealousy.

Peter was posed by her side. He had agreed willingly to the proposal even before he knew who his partner would be. He was a little anxious only in case any of his fellow explorers should come along.

Randers peered into the reflex hood of his Rolleiflex. 'If you could look up a little, Mr Peter … that is good. Thank you.' He cranked the lever.

'You are now acting the first sight of the promised land?' I asked sourly.

'Oh, nao, Col. This is quite different.' He squinted into the hood again.

'I can't see any difference.'

I looked at the other Finnish girl and shrugged my shoulders. She grinned, revealing a steel tooth up on the left side, next to the eye-tooth. Actually she was quite handsome in a coarse way. Strong figure; high complexion; curly hair of middling brown, probably scratchy. She spoke German and her name was Ilse.

'Does this Spartapol thing appeal to you?' I asked her.

'I don't know much about it. I think it would be quite interesting.'

'Yes, but would you want to go to such a camp for your holiday?'

'Perhaps. It would be quite interesting, I think.'

'More interesting than going somewhere on your own, with a friend?'

'That is nice, too.'

We weren't getting very far.

Randers looked up. He called to Ilse. 'Would Miss Pori now please change into maidenly clothing?'

Ilse passed the message on in Finnish and the little one trotted away. After a moment Ilse followed. Peter lit a cigarette.

I said, 'You ought to get one of them drilling with shovels, or something.'

'What do you mean, Col?'

'Traditional Strength-through-Joy image. Or was that labour camps?'

'You are saying nonsense.'

'Ignore him,' said Peter. 'He's jealous because you didn't ask him, that's all.'

'I'm too old,' I said. 'They told me.'

Randers was unshipping the Rollei from its ever-ready case. 'I will change to colour-film in case we print the brochure in colour,' he announced.

I went over and sat by Peter.

'What's eating you?' he murmured. 'We've a marvellous opening here if only you'd stop being so bloody crotchety.'

'Sorry. But aren't there language difficulties? The little one doesn't seem to speak either English or German. My Finno-Ugrian's a bit rusty.'

'Love will find a way. Her name's Maia.'

'The other one's Ilse.' I lowered my voice. 'By the way, I did some research into the identity of your friend in the fo'c'sle.'

'Oh yes. Who is it?'

'Somebody called Williams, Harry Williams. Oddly enough I'd heard of him before. He was a celebrated mining chap in Spitsbergen. He must have wanted to come back to be buried. Very romantic.'

'It is, rather.'

'That's not all. He died in Exaltacion, Bolivia.'

'Death in Exaltation! That's marvellous.'

'It would make a nice title,' I agreed. 'I'm always getting good titles. Trouble is I never sit down and write anything to fit them.'

'You're a writer, then?'

'In a way. Not very successful.'

'I'm supposed to write the account of the expedition. I do History, you see. Are you on the trip looking for material?'

'Not specifically.'

'What are you on it for, then? It's not everyone's idea of a holiday if you don't mind me saying so.'

'That's the trouble. I don't really know. Mainly I'm doing an errand for a pal of mine who runs a little travel agency. He's called Peregrine Potter. Honestly. There may be something else too. I'll tell you later.'

The girls were coming back. The first glimpse of little Maia almost took my breath away. She had changed into a simple linen skirt, bright red, and a white thing like a high-necked pullover only in some soft, thinner stuff that clung gently to her figure.

'Now don't forget,' whispered Peter, 'be nicer to them and we'll be all right tonight. I feel it.'

'…on to the hatch-top for the first one, please,' Randers was instructing.

Maia stepped by me, laughing as Peter made an elaborate bow. Her teeth were tiny and square and her eyes were still the colour of Pears Soap. Her legs were bare and brown and slender and as she clambered on to the hatch-cover I saw the pale skin behind the knees and a glimpse of cool shadowy thigh above.

I rejoined Ilse at the rail. It was time to make conversation. 'And whereabouts in Finland,' I said heavily 'do you live?'

By tea-time, I'd learned that they lived in the north of Finland, a town called Rovaniemi; that Ilse was a teacher and little Maia, astonishingly, a gym instructress. In exchange I'd vouchsafed that Peter went to Cambridge and I was a writer. (It didn't make much impression. Maybe I used the wrong word.) We had also agreed that it was pleasant in the sun though still a little cold, that English cigarettes cost more than Finnish, and that we would be in Longyear in the morning. I'd managed to do without hunting for a shilling to show the picture of our dear young Queen.

Finally Randers said he was finished. As we drifted away, leaving him to pack up his equipment, Peter said, 'While you've been doing whatever you've been doing, I've been busy. I've made us a date for this evening. Up in our ladies' chamber.'

'Jolly good,' I said, trying to sound as if I meant it.

'The little thing's quite pretty, isn't she?' He added charitably, 'Yours would be the better lay, though.'

CHAPTER NINETEEN

In our cabin Randers was writing a letter. He stopped as I came in.

'Col?'

'Mm?'

'Can I say something to you?'

'Of course. What is it?'

'Col, what is the matter? Why are you so unfriendly at once?'

'I don't know what you're talking about.'

'You must knao. What you have said about Strength by Joy, and such things. Then after the photographing you have all avoided me. What is the reason?'

'Oh, for God's sake, we just happened to drift away together. There was nothing deliberate.'

'Why should you want to befriend the second-class girls? They are not interesting.'

'Blimey, who introduced the second-class girls in the first place?'

'I am upset, Col. I feel you are *suspicious* all the time. Is it the sheem you do not like? I am sorry if it has disturbed your plans, but I have tried to warn you.'

I sat down on my bunk. 'All right, I'll tell you. What I don't understand is why you are involved the way you are. What is there in it for you? I mean, I thought you were a travel agent like us. Why aren't you on Potter's side?'

Randers sighed heavily. 'I must tell you something, Col. Perhaps I should have said it before. I have had my little bureau in West Berlin for four years. It has never made very much money. Ultimately, last year I have lost twenty thousand D-Marks.'

'I'm awfully sorry. I had no idea…'

'Please, how could you? Nao, things have not been too well. The hotels put in their own travel bureaux. The airlines all open their own offices in the city. I have lost the account I had with a big firm…'

'I'm sorry.'

'But you knao I have this old interest in Spitsbergen. Along comes the Dr Bland and his *Verband*. He is an old client of mine. They have this Spartapol sheem. We talk about it. I discover what they intend has very little to do with what Mr Potter and I have contemplated. But, you see — they offer me a job. A good job.'

'Ah.'

'It is to be the *chef de buro* — how do you say that? Never mind. It is to look after the office, which will be in Berlin as we hope ultimately to have young people from East Germany. Also I will arrange the travel and will be in charge of the information to the newspapers and so on.'

'The Front Man, in fact?'

'Please?'

'Nothing, nothing. If you like it, I'm very glad for you.'

The date wasn't a great success. We went after dinner. Up in the little ladies' cabin the dominant impression was of varnished woodwork. A varnished seat ran round three sides, a varnished table occupied half the remaining floor space. But there was a faintly feminine air brought about by traces of the girls' occupation: a couple of magazines, a Finnish newspaper, a bag of oranges, a folded silk square and a cheap box camera in the kind of leatherette pouch that only a woman would bother with.

'Our little home,' said Ilse.

Maia was sitting writing in what looked like a desk diary. She was wearing a pair of funny little steel-rimmed spectacles with round lenses like a child's, which she clawed off with an appropriately childish gesture as we entered. Her hands were small, smooth and exquisitely neat. Her eyes, I decided, were not so much the colour of Pears Soap as of those pale unmounted cairngorms you see sometimes in jewellers' windows. She spoke in a kind of breathless, rippling way, the ends of her sentences sliding into half-giggles. If I could have understood even a word of it I would probably have been out of love again there and then; as a straight sound effect it was feminine and enticing.

Ilse provided bits of translation from time to time in German and also in a few scraps of English which she now produced. She had undistinguished features. There wasn't anything specifically wrong with them but you wouldn't notice them in a crowd. At close quarters her complexion was rough, though she'd put on some make-up. Her hands were large and red… Why am I cataloguing all this? Because she was still basically, indisputably, attractive, or rather *attracting*. She was the kind of girl who in any community would never lack a boyfriend. As Peter had said, she would be a good lay.

We talked — oh, we talked and talked. I can't remember what it was all about, but again it was that tedious exchange of information that makes up the average transliteral conversation. Peter tackled it with the zest of youth. He tried bits of German and bits of Swedish and borrowed a pencil and wrote words on the back of an envelope. I grew more and more bored and more and more jealous, for he directed his efforts entirely at Maia, while the more fluent German which Ilse and I shared tended to pair us off apart.

I tried once to head the conversation into the matter of Spartapol. How had the approach been made about the pictures? What else had been said? Ilse said that Bland had come up to them out of the blue that morning. He spoke a little Finnish, it seemed. He had asked them how they happened to be going to Svalbard and told them about his scheme. Then he had inquired if it interested them.

And did it?

'You already asked me on the deck this afternoon. Maia is interested because she is a physical education teacher at home. The doctor has said there will be work at the camp every summer for such people. It would be very interesting.' She said something to Maia, who nodded vigorously and smiled at me.

It stabbed me, a smile of irresponsible sweetness. But what potty gym-mistress sentiments underlay it? I gave up. It became evident that the date wasn't going to yield any positive results. To my relief, surreptitious attempts by Peter to divide up the party failed.

I took him up to our saloon for a nightcap.

'Sorry it didn't get more cosy,' I said on the way.

'Can't be helped,' he said, philosophically. 'Anyway, Maia's too nice for a casual fumble. Ilse too, of course.'

'I know. You don't make that kind of girl the first day you meet her! It takes two days.'

In the saloon Randers was sitting on his own, a brandy in front of him. We joined him. It seemed desirable to have a Let's-be-nice-to-Randers phase.

He said, 'You have missed the excitement.'

'What excitement?'

'The Russian settlement at Barentsburg. We have passed it about half an hour since.'

I hadn't been following progress. The *Bellsund* was steaming closer to land now, and in smoother waters. Through the saloon windows I could see a dark shoreline with black-streaked snowy mountains rising continuously behind.

'We have turned off the sea,' said Randers, in nice un-nautical language, 'and are going up the Isfjorden towards Longyear City. Through glasses you could see the Russian houses and their little railway on the mountainside. You could not see any life.'

'Perhaps they'd gone to bed.'

'Perhaps.' He lowered his voice. 'The Terrible Americans were astounded. They had never been so close to Russians in their life. They were looking to see if there were atom-rockets there! The woman, she kept saying, "I be goddamned, I be goddamned."' He drank up his brandy. 'Now I must go to bed also. Mr Peter, I hope to see you again tomorrow. If not, may I wish you a stirring expedition!'

CHAPTER TWENTY

When he'd gone I said to Peter, I'd better tell you something. I've been meaning to for some time. You know Randers, and though you haven't met Bland you must have seen him around. He's the cove with the green-tinted specs who looks as if he lives on All-Bran and spinach. Very fit. They're in this Spartapol thing together.'

I ran through the whole story in brief, including the Mystery Visitor, but leaving aside the corpse in the fo'c'sle for the time being. Dancer, I didn't mention at all.

At the end Peter said, 'It seems fairly straightforward. Except for the chap who called at your office, and I suppose he could have seen a proof copy of the brochure.'

'We thought of that. There were some sent out, but only within the trade. Not to the general public.'

'Would Randers have had one?'

'We thought of that, too. Yes, he would.'

'Isn't that the answer? He sent it on to this crowd he's with now and one of them took it up, not knowing that Bland was already going over your head to Edinburgh.'

'Could be. There are one or two more minor mysteries, though. There's our friend in the luggage hold, the late Mr Williams. I'm sure Bland is involved there somehow. I happened to get the plane from Oslo that carried the coffin. Bland was travelling on it, too, as if he were keeping an eye on things. I mean, why didn't he come the same way as Randers, which was through Stockholm and Narvik? He said he was finding out about air travel for his young louts. Yet Randers is supposed to be the travel expert.'

Peter didn't look very impressed. I struggled on.

'Then there's a long-playing gramophone record in Randers's luggage which he says Bland asked him to bring from Germany. Why couldn't Bland have brought it himself? I'm beginning to think he hasn't been in Germany lately — perhaps not for a long time. That might explain why Randers got in such a muddle — you know, working with us at first and then suddenly trying to put us off. Bland could have suddenly got in touch … I bet he was the Mystery Caller, snooping round to see what sort of an organization we were.'

Peter yawned.

'He's got the green lenses and a slight American intonation, if you listen carefully, like the little girl described. Anyway, why take a Berlioz record to the North Pole? What's the point?'

'Honestly, I think it's a bit thin.'

'I know it wouldn't do for John Buchan. But I do get the feeling that someone's trying to nudge us out of a corner of the Arctic that should be for ever England. Why the haste to complete the deal? They can't do anything this year now.'

Peter yawned a second time. 'I don't know. Write it as a thriller. I'll buy the paperback when it comes out.'

I'd been nerving myself to ask him if he'd consider leaving the expedition and staying aboard the *Bellsund*. It was a preposterous idea, of course, but it had become a very tempting one: I yearned for an ally. Now it fell into perspective.

I said, 'The trouble with youth today is that it's got no sense of adventure.'

'I know. It's the Welfare State. We need some air raids.' He stood up.

'When are you off?'

'We go ashore tomorrow and stay the night in some shed. Go on in the Governor's boat the next day.'

'See you around,' I said.

I sat on in the saloon and had one more drink. The steward asked if it would be the last, as he wanted to close up. I said it would. I wanted to think. For all Peter's scepticism I felt sure that something was fishy. I respected the feeling because normally I was easily fobbed off. I'd lasted three months as a reporter, at the end of which time the news editor had said not unkindly, 'Panton, if Jesus Christ had told you there was No Story when He walked on the water, you'd have believed Him.'

Admittedly, there wasn't much to support my instincts. The circumstances I had given Peter. What else? Surely the whole Spartapol scheme was suspiciously unrealistic in that it would be able to function for such a brief season each year. The *Bellsund* plied little more than two months, because — someone had said — insurance costs for a scheduled passenger service earlier or later in the short Arctic summer would be too heavy. Even with air transport I couldn't see how the place could operate for more than four months.

Then Randers's behaviour didn't satisfy me as a writer. Behind the clown face he was wary. Even the references to Miss Penywern no longer had spontaneity. They struck me as deliberate devices to allay suspicion. With Bland, to be honest, it was plain dislike. We'd got off on the wrong foot at the start. Finally, I felt a curious sense of responsibility to Rogerson, as if he'd picked me, against all advice, for the school First Fifteen. I didn't particularly want to play, but it was nice to be asked. Next day a decision would have to be made. If I wanted to impede the deal going through I'd have to cable from Longyear. If not I ought to cable an All Clear. It was as simple as that.

I went on deck for a last blow before trying to sleep. It was that milky timeless Arctic midnight. Bland was looking at the shore through a little monocular glass. He heard me and beckoned. He handed me the glass and nodded to the shore. We were passing another cluster of buildings huddled against the flank of mountains which seemed to rise directly from the water.

'Our friends,' said Bland in a tone of voice which I interpreted as half banter, half a gentle test of reactions.

The place was Grumantbyen, second of the Russian mining townships. Again there was no sign of life.

I said, 'It seems the Americans believe they are building rocket sites from which to aim H-Bombs at Long Island. They can't get over it.'

'They are mad.'

'You don't distrust the Russians, then?'

'I trust them no more and no less than any other nation. I am a German, Mr Panton. To be exact, a Bavarian, for in these matters it seems we are increasingly exact…'

He paused for a moment. 'It would be quite logical for the Russians to build fortifications in the Arctic, including rocket launching installations. But not here on Svalbard. Everything is open to inspection by the Norwegian authorities. Have you any idea how big a rocket launching platform is, Mr Panton?'

I shook my head.

'I can tell you it would be difficult to hide such a thing from an inquisitive inspector of mines. No, if they wish to train missiles on the United States from the north they have only to build the platforms on their own islands, such as Novaya Zemlaya. You can be sure they have done so.'

I peered through the monocular. The buildings swam into vision, clear and near and yet toy-like. I tried to imagine what it was like inside them. Who were these Russians who spent their lives in isolation, marooned on an outpost of Europe? Did they come from the old-fashioned capitalist motives of the Norwegian miners who worked in Longyear and Ny Alesund — to make enough money in a few years to buy a house and start a business back in civilization? Or were they just drafted at random by the great clanking wheels of Soviet bureaucracy?

I said, 'Do they volunteer to come here or are they sent?'

'They come because they choose to. Would you send anyone against his will to a place from where he might escape to the West and tell stories about slave labour?'

'I suppose not.'

'The life is hard over there' — Bland pointed to the receding settlement. 'Long hours, much work, living in barracks. But so is life everywhere in Russia. There is no harm in hardness. The West is too soft.'

'I like it that way. What would you have us do? Throw away all the washing machines and television sets? Abolish central heating and Mediterranean holidays?'

Bland frowned. 'Yes, if you like. In a few hours we arrive at Longyear. Good night.'

I said quickly, 'I'm sorry for being flippant. It was silly. I'm interested in what you say.'

He hesitated. 'It is all right, Mr Panton. You must excuse me. It is what you call a hobby-horse of mine. Look, for you in England it is simple. You have enormous lands over the sea. Canada, Australia, Africa. They need millions of new people. New European people, you understand? You should send them from England. I wish we had somewhere we could send people from Germany.'

'Most of those who want to emigrate manage it. There are all sorts of schemes to help them.'

'A few thousand. Nothing.'

'The others don't want to go. You can't force people to emigrate if they don't want to.'

'Why not? People do not know what they want, Mr Panton. They would be happier if they were told what to do and where to go. Oh, there would be an outcry at first. But in the end they would accept it.'

I was silent.

'For us, Mr Panton, there are no dominions overseas. There is only Germany, and half of her is with the Russians. There is nowhere to provide —' he strove for a word — 'nowhere to provide a challenge. Our new army is an army of mother's boys. They have rights and committees. What does a soldier want with rights and committees?'

Everything he can get out of them, I thought privately. I said, 'Will your organization have a uniform?'

Bland said quietly, 'I know what you are thinking. The answer is, of course not. We have had enough of that, all of us. The only uniform will be wind-jacket, ski-clothing, climbing boots and red in the cheeks. Randers has told you we will try and bring young people from the East Zone here?'

'Yes, he did.'

'And after that from Austria and France and Czechoslovakia and England — and from Russia. Why not? Up here in Svalbard, Mr Panton, the West and the East lived together long before any so-called thaw in the Cold War. Even when Stalin was alive the Russians and Norwegians would meet in friendship. Up here we will bring the two halves of Germany together, away from the quarrelling politicians. And then the two halves of all Europe, Mr Panton. Here will be the cradle of a New Europa! Are you not —' he groped for a word — 'are you not stirred?'

He didn't really expect an answer. He was looking into some limitless distance, standing quite still in that enviable, alarming repose that he commanded.

CHAPTER TWENTY-ONE

Longyear City was not prepossessing at first sight, which was through the saloon windows at breakfast. The *Bellsund* was tied up at a massive timber landing stage. Beyond it there was the usual waterfront litter. Two big American lorries, painted orange, came bumping along a dirt road and drew up. The ground rose to a low bluff surmounted by two rather handsome buildings, one with a flagpole, and a good deal of unhandsome chicken wire and corrugated iron.

I finished breakfast quickly. I had an urge to get ashore on my own and walk and think and visit the cable office in peace. I slipped out of the saloon and went down the gangway. One of the lorries was just leaving.

The driver leaned out of his window. 'Want a lift?'

I said, 'Fine. Thanks,' and scrambled up.

'You English?'

'Yes. You sound American.'

'No, I'm Norwegian. Worked in Canada twelve years. Was in the Canadian army too. What you doing in this dump?'

'Just looking.'

'Uh-huh.' He accepted that. 'It's not a bad dump. I've been here nine years. It's all right. Where you from?'

'London.'

'Uh-huh. You know Middlesbrough? I was in Middlesbrough in the war. That's a goddam town.'

'I bet it is.'

'Had a good time in Middlesbrough. Plenty fun. Where do you want?'

'The cable office if you're going near.'

'The radio station, you mean. It's up the hill there. But it's closed till twelve noon, I guess.'

'Anywhere, then.'

The lorry bounced up to the top of the bluff, past the two good-looking buildings. The one with the flagpole was the Governor's residence, said the driver. Stretching ahead was a long broad valley between steep slopes pitted with snow. A mile further on was a formation of tall buildings like barrack blocks, with high pitched roofs. On the other side of the valley was another settlement. I recognized the scene as the one in Rogerson's picture. Only now the viewpoint was different, and it was prosaic day instead of romantic night. The lorry pulled up outside an imposing brick-built edifice of civic character.

'Post Office,' said the driver. 'Restaurant. Pictures. The city centre, huh? The shop is across the other side. See you.' He drove off.

The post office was also closed, but there was a pad of telegraph forms hanging outside. I tore off a couple and went on my way. There was hardly a soul in sight. The orange lorry was driving dustily on up the valley to a distant installation that was obviously a mine. There was another one, nearer, across the valley: a tunnel mouth high up on the hillside, huts and machinery clinging around it, a cable railway down to the valley. As I watched, a tiny wagon was crawling up and another crawling down.

I took the path across to the other settlement. Nearing the centre of the valley the way grew increasingly swampy. My old suede shoes began to squelch ominously. I transferred to the top of a kind of wooden catwalk enclosing pipes and cables. The air was fresh, with a chill breeze blowing down the valley. At its distant head gleamed the white ramparts of a glacier.

The shop, for God's sake, was closed as well. But a notice on the door said that it would be open within half an hour. To while away the time I walked round the settlement. It turned out to be a bit of a slum. There was nothing wrong with the houses, high and solid with double windows against the cold. But behind them the rubbish lay thick on the ground. There was a musty smell of rotting vegetables. I found myself walking on potato peelings and cinders. Cigarette packets and old papers were littered about. Behind one hut was a damp pile of Scandinavian naturist magazines with their clinical pictures of undepilated nudes. I remembered Rogerson telling me that many of the miners lived celibate lives in barrack-like dormitories, though two children playing with an oil-drum a little way away, and a line of nappies fluttering near the store, were evidence that there were now some families as well. I learned later that Longyear citizens weren't consciously unhygienic. From October to April the snow swallowed up and obliterated any rubbish that was thrown out. In summer, when most of them were away, the refuse came to light again.

In the shop I bought a thick fisherman's jersey and a pair of ski boots. Everything was absurdly cheap.

Down at the distant landing-stage a derrick unwound midget cargo from a midget *Bellsund*. The ant-like figures of explorers toiled to and fro with their stores. Next to the steamer, only slightly smaller, was the Governor's motor vessel. Out in the fjord was moored the *Harriet*, the toy yacht of gleaming white that would take the Americans on their hunting trip.

In my new ski boots and jersey I had scrambled up the hillside until I was high above Longyear, panting and hot. I walked along a rough shoulder of the mountain, letting the breeze cool me. The turf was yielding but dead, like an old sponge. Here and there a scruffy grass grew, dotted with tiny pink and white flowers. I came to some old graves and an untidy cairn of stones. I lit a cigarette and sat down.

For the umpteenth time the familiar muddle revolved in my head: Spartapol, Randers, the late Williams, Bland, Dancer, the Mystery Caller, Berlioz … I'd rather neglected Berlioz. Why should Bland want that?

Answer: it could be a present for someone — one of the officials, perhaps. Bland was establishing a little good-will. He probably had cigars and cameras tucked away in his baggage to the same end. That was the trouble. Half the time everything seemed to have a valid explanation and half the time it seemed all wrong. I wished the hell I'd never got involved. I found the telegraph forms and smoothed them out. On the first one I wrote a get-out which I judged was not too abject:

POTTER UNLIKELY TO BE INTERESTED FURTHER STOP SUGGEST SPARTAPOL OFFER PROCEED

On the second form I wrote:

SPARTAPOL SMELLS STOP SUGGEST YOU OPPOSE OFFER STRONGEST STOP CONTACT ME NY ALESUND STOP DID YOU KNOW A HARRY WILLIAMS QUERY

That was a lot more words, which was a factor to be considered. An absurd thing was that I was running short of money. I'd cashed all my travellers' cheques except one in Bodø. I could probably change it on the boat. In cash I had about eighty kroner, or four pounds.

I addressed both cables to Rogerson, signed them and put them away. One in my left-hand trouser pocket, one in my right. Down below there was brisk traffic between ship and settlement.

The French climbers strode purposefully along the road by the post office. Further along two unmistakable little figures headed for the shop. Maia's fair head bobbed level with Ilse's shoulder. Their ever-trousered legs twinkled in step. I toyed with the idea of catching them up but made no move. Finally I recognized Peter approaching from the ship with two other explorers. I slithered and trotted down to them.

CHAPTER TWENTY-TWO

We've been seeing the Governor,' said Peter. 'Or rather, his deputy. The man himself is on leave.'

'All of you?'

'No, just the Leader and the Second Leader and the head stone-chipper. And me because I'm the official scribe. They thought I ought to be present to describe negotiations.'

'Everything work out all right?'

'Yes, thanks. The Governor's launch is taking us tomorrow, all as arranged. Everyone very charming.'

We were back at the civic-style building. The explorers went into the post office. I waited outside, fingering the cable forms in my pockets and looking around. It was quite a place to find in so remote an outpost. Lots of good woodwork. Massive glass doors into the restaurant. Wide stairs up to what was evidently a cinema. *Mogambo*, announced a poster, med Clark Gable og Ava Gardner.

'How about a drink?' said one of the explorers as they reappeared. He said it in clipped military accents I didn't much care for, but the suggestion was the nicest I'd heard all day. I looked hopefully at Peter.

'I don't suppose the Leader would approve,' he said. 'So let's.'

'Hooray.'

Peter said, 'You all know Colin, do you? He's in the first class but not a bad chap. This is Gregg' — the military one — 'and Skinner.' They smiled in greeting and I suddenly liked them much more. We trooped through the glass doors and across the big room within. One side had a counter running the length of the room, with bar-type fittings and lots of glasses in view.

'Steady, chaps,' said Gregg. 'They don't serve at the bar. Pray let us be seated.'

Peter said, 'Gregg's been here before, as he's never tired of telling everyone.'

'Quiet, boy.'

We sat down at a table. 'The beer,' said Gregg, 'is good here. But watch it. It's strong. They brew it especially for the miners. It's also jolly cheap, so you can have this round on me.'

A hefty waitress in black hovered over us. Gregg ordered four beers. She padded away and presently came back with four enormous dark bottles and some glasses. We poured out carefully.

'First today,' said Gregg. 'All that shifting of stuff is thirsty work. Cheers.'

The beer had a nice clean taste and lots of body; not much like English beer, but nearer to it than the usual windy lager. I discovered an agreeable thirst.

'Are you on holiday, or what?' asked Skinner.

'Partly business, partly holiday.' I had been hoping not to have to produce credentials any more.

'He's reconnoitring the place for a holiday camp,' said Peter. 'Billy Butlin wants to move in. It'll be quieter than Filey.'

'Shut up,' said Skinner. 'Are you really in the travel business?'

'I suppose so. At least I'm representing an agency at the moment. I do other things as well.' (That old inferiority complex — what's wrong with the travel business?) I explained Potter's original scheme briefly.

'I don't think it would work,' said Gregg flatly. 'I've been in Svalbard before, as I never tire of pointing out to everyone. It's okay for our kind of thing but it would be Harry Grimmers for ordinary civilians.'

Peter stuck out his tongue. 'Just because you're in the army you think anyone who isn't is so wet they have to be taken to the lavatory.'

'Balls.'

'It would be mainly for specialist interests,' I explained. 'You know — birdwatchers and climbers and fairly rugged schoolteachers. But it looks as if it's all falling through now.'

'Why's that?'

'Mainly because those Germans who are on the trip have outbid us.'

'Do you mean that alert-looking chappie in the green suit?'

'He's one of them.'

'He was sounding out the Leader last night, I gather. He's interested in some sort of youth stunt up in Krossfjorden.'

'That's right. His name's Bland. What was he trying to find out?'

'Oh, you know. The kind of co-operation we get from the authorities here, and how much they interfere. What sort of jobs the Polar Institute likes having done. That sort of thing. Seemed quite a good chap according to the Leader. Who is he, exactly?'

'An outdoor type. Interested in a kind of Strength-through-Joy scheme to give European youth a bit of hard living in the Arctic. You know, knickers and vests at dawn.'

'Good idea,' said Gregg. His face went professionally stern.

'Oh sure,' I said. 'Providing it doesn't turn out the way it did last time anyone preached that particular sermon. How about some more of those big cool bottles?'

I caught the waitress's eye, and another load arrived. Two more explorers were drifting in, so the order went up to six.

Something was nagging away in the back of my mind. It was Gregg's question about Bland — 'Who is he exactly?' I realized how little I knew.

I talked to Gregg a bit more. He was the Second Leader of the expedition, as Peter called him. He had one of those common military faces, lean and obedient and never relaxing too much, in case its owner shouldn't seem alert. Brown hair, short and crinkly, little brown moustache. He was a lieutenant in a training unit, Royal Engineers.

'My old corps.' I told him.

'Really? You were a sapper?' He was delighted.

'Literally. In rank as well as calling.' I named the company, which was an honourable one. He was duly impressed.

He said, 'I'd like to get attached to the Parachute Regiment if I can. Or better still, the Special Air Service.'

'Why?'

'More exciting, I suppose.'

I didn't pursue the matter. It was difficult to explain exactly how I felt, especially to him. I really ought to be doing something about those cables.

Another round of beers arrived. The bottles were beginning to cluster impressively on the table, or rather, tables. The school was now nine strong. A few local denizens had also arrived. They gave us a cursory look and settled to their own affairs. A party of four lined up a dozen bottles on a table and began to play cards. Others read letters and papers that had presumably arrived on the *Bellsund*. They wore denims, T-shirts, hide boots. One had a miner's helmet on his shoulder, another his wrist in yellowing plaster.

There might have been a move at this stage if the French climbers hadn't come in. There were shouts of entente cordiale and in no time at all more beer.

'We wish you Good 'Ardship,' the Frenchmen said, raising their glasses.

'We wish you bloody 'ard time, too,' said the explorers cordially.

I was really making a strong-willed effort to go. I'd paid my second round, and it cost sixteen kroner this time.

'Got to get back to the ship, chaps? I said to no one in particular. 'There's a thing I've got to do.'

'You can't,' said one of the explorers.

'Why not? Who says I can't?'

''Cos the ship isn't there, that's why. It's gone round to the coaling wharf to fuel up. Won't be back till after one. They warned us. Didn't you hear?'

Inevitably a rugger scrum formed up. They knocked three bottles over. Someone lined up the surviving empties and began to drill them. It was embarrassingly hearty.

'Then they went to Trieste with Thirteen Brigade, you know,' said Gregg. He was still on about my old company.

'Did they? Well, if you'll excuse…'

'Yes, came under my old man, actually. He was Chief Engineer out there until he retired in '47.'

'Look, I must…'

'I went out there for the summer hols one year. Let's see, it must have been '46, the year before he came back. No, wait a minute! It *was* '47. He finished that Christmas.' He was one of those people who have a terrible desire to impart information.

My friend the lorry driver had turned up. 'You must have a beer,' I said carefully. 'You must have a beer with me.' I brandished two fingers at the waitress.

'Hey, Mac, that could be misunderstood.'

'I was forgetting. I've been living in the wrong world too long.' With mild surprise I found I couldn't quite cope with 'wrong world'. I took it slowly but it still came out 'wong wrorld'. 'I mean I've been out of touch with the dingity of labour. You know what the dingity of labour is…?'

We shambled off eventually, singing. I was clutching an unopened bottle of beer to take back and hoard away, like a squirrel. But at the radio station I remembered to wheel away from the party. At the counter I fumbled with the cable forms. Right or left? Did I choose, did I know? Don't ask me. The charge was seventeen kroner. I kept a grim hold of the bottle and fumbled with grubby little notes and coins until finally the man politely helped himself. There was just enough.

Somewhere near the boat I fished out the cable I still had left and tore it into little bits. It said 'POTTER UNLIKELY TO BE INTERESTED FURTHER…' The die was cast.

CHAPTER TWENTY-THREE

At dinner I picked at the meat balls and potatoes, barely tasted the stewed fruit, and gulped down three cups of coffee. On deck a fresh cold wind blew from the open sea and the attendant seabirds honked and squeaked as they waited for scraps. Mechanically I identified an Arctic tern, two skuas, and the usual crowd of gulls and guillemots. The *Bellsund* was chugging down Isfjorden again, heading for the open sea. The next call was at Ny Alesund.

She seemed oddly quiet and empty now. The Cambridge explorers, the French climbers, the nurses and officials, had all remained in Longyear. The incredible Americans had sailed off on their hunting trip — twice. Once for the cameraman, once in reality, to the cheers and applause of drunken explorers. I had slept for a while, disastrously, waking with a headache and a mouth like a birdcage. Then our turn had come. The explorers and the Frenchmen had come to the landing stage to see us off, stout boots planted firmly on the wooden planking. Peter had waved goodbye ruefully and blown a kiss to Maia.

The *Bellsund's* trail of smoke streamed away from the single grubby funnel. The matt black coal heaps of Longyear receded in the distance. The wire cable of the log revolved patiently on its bearings. I filled up with cold air and on the impulse went up to the girls' little day-cabin.

'Come in,' said Ilse. Both of them were smiling. 'You are feeling better?'

'How do you mean?' It was warm and faintly feminine inside.

'We saw you with the students.'

'Oh, that!' I pushed my hand through my hair and ran my tongue round my mouth. Maia showed her little square teeth with delight. 'What did you do?' I asked.

'We walked a lot. All round the town.' Ilse stressed the word '*stat*' ironically. 'We saw the hospital, the memorial from the war, the shop, the Governor's house and his dogs — did you see his dogs?'

'No. I believe I smelled them, though.'

'They are sledge-dogs just like you see in films. And barking and barking. Then we walked right up the valley to the far coal mine.'

I said how nice that must have been. I was watching Maia. One leg was crossed over the other, stretching trousers tight across a thigh as round and tapering as a Peynet girl's. In the warm cabin she had discarded the anorak and thick pullover again for the little fluffy white garment she'd worn for the photography session.

I said, 'Do you like my jersey? Bought it in the shop.'

They nodded their heads vigorously and Ilse fingered the wool. It was fine and warm, she opined. She was wearing a crumpled wool shirt buttoned tightly across full breasts. The sleeves were rolled up, and her forearms were muscular and hard. Maia's sleeves were pushed back from round, soft, honey-golden forearms, pale on the inside. She was scratching away in the same diary or notebook as the previous evening, hooking on the same quaint little specs.

'Is that a diary?' I said.

'Yes, it is a record of our journey. Every night Maia writes down everything we have done during the day. In the winter we often read through it and laugh.'

'You've done it before, then?'

'Oh yes. Last year we have gone to Finmark for our holiday and Maia kept a diary. It was only a small book. This year there is room for more.'

'A good idea.'

There was a lull. Maia bent her head again. She wrote quickly, neatly, in tiny cramped characters. The tip of a pink tongue peeped from between her lips.

'So Peter is left behind in Longyear?' I observed. 'Maia is sad?'

Ilse grinned metallically and translated. Maia, I was encouraged to note, only shrugged and went on writing.

'She is writing about the departure now,' said Ilse. 'She will soon be finished.'

Maia straightened up and looked at her handiwork critically. Ilse bent over to read it with her, her coarse dark hair close to Maia's shining golden. Her lips moved as she read. She laughed twice and once Maia joined in, and they exchanged a few words in Finnish.

'That is good,' she said finally, in German.

'What does she say?'

'Oh, about all we have seen in Longyear. The things we told you of, and the students moving their things off the boat, and about you!'

'What about me?'

She beamed. 'That you were a little *blau*.' She passed the joke on to Maia, who smiled again and stabbed me anew. As if to turn the blade in the wound she clawed off the absurd spectacles.

Ilse said, 'At Ny Alesund we must all explore together. It will be more fun.'

I agreed enthusiastically, only remembering as I left that I might have other things to do there now. Maia closed her journal and snapped a thick elastic band round it.

Randers was also writing away at something. It turned out to be a letter to Miss Penywern,

'I have told her about you and the celebration with the students from Cambridge,' he announced. 'She will be very amused.'

'Good,' I said. 'I'm sorry I didn't see you much today.'

'Oh please do not mention it, dear fellow, I think it must have been great fun. I would have come and sought you all out myself, but the Dr Bland and I had much to do. We have seen the Governor's deputy, you knao, and consulted at the hospital about medical emergencies etcetera.'

'Randers, about the scheme and everything…'

'Yes?'

'I've decided that it's extremely unlikely that Mr Potter will still be interested in Spitsbergen, and that it would be unfair to stand in your way any longer…'

'Oh, Col, that is very fine of you, though I am sorry it has worked out so. I will inform the Dr Bland.'

'Whoops. Wait a minute. I was going to add that I think it's only proper, however, that I should have a look at the place first. After all, I've come all this way…'

'Of course, of course. I will speak to the Dr Bland. I am sure it will be all right. I think we are going over tomorrow from Ny Alesund. It is two or three hours in a motorboat, you understand.'

But it was not all right by Dr Bland. He took the unprecedented step of coming back with Randers to our cabin.

'Mr Panton, of course we will be very pleased if you will look over the site we have in mind for our scheme. However, I do not think it will be possible tomorrow. I will tell you why in a second. I would suggest that you come on Sunday when the *Bellsund* returns to Ny Alesund on her way south. We will have from early morning then until six thirty p.m. when she sails again. That will give us enough time to make the journey and back. I shall suggest you get up very early indeed! We should try and set out about five a.m.'

This was all very well. I didn't want to wait another forty-eight hours before making the excursion, even if I didn't quite know what I was going to do when I made it. I opened my mouth to object.

'Moment, moment!' Bland was unfolding a map of the archipelago. 'Here is Ny Alesund,' he said. 'And here in the next fjord — see — is our probable camp site at Holyroodhamna. It is necessary to allow two hours by motorboat, perhaps two and a half. Now tomorrow it is impossible to start early. You could not be back by sailing time.'

'Why can't we start early?' I'm bad at getting up but I was prepared to make a special effort, just once.

'Did you know a deputy inspector of mines had come aboard at Longyear?'

'I saw someone at the Captain's table. I didn't know who it was.'

'Yes, well he is representing the Governor. He is travelling with us to Ny Alesund for a little ceremony tomorrow morning, and I thought it would be —' he hesitated — 'I thought it would be correct if we all attended. The authorities would be pleased.'

I could guess what was coming.

'Aboard this ship,' said Bland, 'is the body of a mining engineer who was one of the pioneers in this part of the world fifty years ago. He has willed to be buried here, and the funeral will be tomorrow morning at eleven o'clock.'

'I see.'

'It means we cannot set out for our camp until twelve noon at the earliest. To try and be back for six thirty p.m. would be madness. And I am sure Mr Peregrine Potter would wish you to experience the remainder of the *Bellsund's* voyage, to Magdalene-fjorden and Danish Island. It is very romantic.'

'Perhaps.' I'd been taken off balance.

'So. It is settled. Tomorrow Mr Randers and I will possibly go across after the ceremony. We have some heavy stores to move there. We could have lunch before we go.'

'Good idea,' said Randers dutifully.

'We will not need to return until midnight to sleep in our luxury apartment in Ny Alesund!' God, he was even unbending to the extent of a joke. 'Then on Sunday *you* shall see our new Sparta, Mr Panton.'

Thanks very much for nothing. But even as I lay in bed wishing I didn't feel so restless and kicking myself for being so docile, I knew that being taken on a Cooks Tour by Bland would have been pretty valueless. There was still time to fix something better. What, though?

'Randers?'

He made a sort of croak.

'Randers!'

'What is it, Col? I am sleeping.'

'What does Bland do?'

'He is the director of Spartapol. You know that.'

'No, what else does he do? What's his job? What's he a doctor *of*?'

'I am not sure. Science, I think. He has many interests, you knao.'

'Was he in England a little while ago?'

'He was to Edinburgh to see Ferguson, Roberts and Holburn S.S.C…'

'Yes, yes, you told me.'

'Col, I'm tired. Can we not talk in the morning?'

'Oh, all right.'

When it was one a.m. and I still couldn't sleep, I got up stealthily and crept out of the cabin with sweater, slacks and socks in my hand. Randers was whiffling peacefully. I pulled the clothes on over my pyjamas and padded along down to the second-class quarters. At the foot of the companionway there were a couple of closed doors I hadn't noticed before. Obviously they were the smaller cabins. I listened carefully and decided I could hear breathing noises behind one of them. That would be the girls. In the other direction was the saloon-like room through which Peter had taken me. Beyond it, the big cabin which the explorers had occupied. Now it was empty, the bunks freshly made up with clean eiderdowns and pillows. At the far end was the bolted fo'c'sle door. It took a little nerve — nonsense, it took a lot of nerve — but I slid back the bolts and reached inside to switch on the light.

The coffin was where it had always been, but, with the departure of the explorer's gear, now stood in splendid isolation, supported off the floor on an improvised bier of timber packing pieces. It reminded me of the little black joke Jessie Blackwell and I had discovered for ourselves on the Forth ferry when I'd once stayed with her in Edinburgh. There was a notice up that listed the single and return fares for everything you could think of, from a horse and trap to a hearse. Right at the end, after 'Hearse' came 'Corpse'. This time there was only the single fare given; it was a shilling, actually.

I was smiling thinly to myself at the recollection when the vision of a dead Dancer suddenly recurred. He was lying with peaked, waxy features in a white coffin. I pulled the door shut and scuttled away.

CHAPTER TWENTY-FOUR

The prospect of Ny Alesund was as appealing as that of Longyear had been grim. Again the settlement was sited on the southern shore of a sheltered fjord, called Kingsbay.

Through the struts of the high landing stage I could see wooden houses painted a faded, weather-beaten blue-grey. Behind them a smooth field of snow rose to a jagged skyline. Along the fjord the foreshore was a bright olive-green; after about a mile the dark clutter of coal mines obtruded. The fjord itself looked two or three miles wide at this point. It was probably more — distances were deceptive in the clear Arctic air. It stretched inland like a great highway, without narrowing, until arbitrarily it was cut off by the mouths of the glaciers which fed it. They gleamed in the distance like cliffs of pale-blue crystal. Across the fjord the inevitable Svalbard horizon of pointed mountains was presided over by a smooth peak which the map identified as Mount Grimaldi. Beyond it lay Krossfjorden and the end of the trail. The sun shone in a pale-blue sky strewn with little white clouds.

After my nocturnal excursion I had slept well, and long; just as well I hadn't to rise at five. It was nine thirty as I wandered ashore. Ilse was standing by the gangway.

'Are you coming for an exploration along the fjord?' she asked. 'We could try and reach the glacier.'

I explained about the funeral ceremony.

She looked comically crestfallen but I didn't find it very funny. Nothing would have been nicer than a seashore ramble with the ladies. Alas, it was necessary to see the late Mr Williams laid to rest.

Ilse was pondering. 'We could go straight afterwards,' she said, brightening. 'What time is it over?'

'By twelve noon at the latest. Probably earlier.'

'Then we will meet here. I will wait from eleven thirty. I will ask for some food to take with us.'

'Excellent,' I said.

The post office and radio station were in the same shabby building. There was no word from Rogerson, but I wasn't really expecting anything yet. The post office side of the business advertised that it was the most northerly in the world. I bought a postcard and addressed it to Jane in New Zealand — the address she'd given me before she left that time. It was peculiarly satisfying to think that it would go from the seventy-ninth parallel in the northern hemisphere to somewhere about the sixtieth in the southern. The only message I could think of was '*Wish you were here.*' I wrote it, and as an afterthought signed it Santa Claus. She'd know my writing. The man franked the card with an enormous purple stamp featuring a polar bear and dropped it in a sack.

CHAPTER TWENTY-FIVE

The grave was shallow, a seven or eight-foot furrow scarcely twelve inches deep. Round it was piled the dusty Svalbard top soil and lumps of frozen clay. The coffin was already in position, draped with a faded Stars and Stripes. On the top rested, touchingly, a little wreath of twisted wire and tiny Svalbard flowers.

'It is not possible to dig any deeper,' whispered the radio officer. 'The earth is frozen too hard.'

We were standing on a wide expanse of spongy, stone-littered turf between the settlement and the mines. One side ran down to the edge of the fjord, sparkling bluely in the sunlight. The other was bordered by a light railway which linked mines and waterfront. A little black engine had come panting from the quayside drawing a single flat-car on which the late Mr Williams had made his last wheeled journey. Six miners wearing their helmets had carried him the remaining two hundred yards.

We weren't a very large party of mourners. From the ship, the captain and the radio officer. The six miners, and a maintenance engineer from the coal company, in a leather jacket. The deputy inspector of mines, wearing a tweed overcoat. Bland. Randers. Myself. The Swedish tourist.

The deputy inspector of mines cleared his throat and stepped forward. He spoke haltingly, his voice sinking at the end of each phrase.

'Though none of us had personal knowledge of him,' translated the radio officer in a whisper, 'this man was one of the pioneers of mining in Svalbard. He first came here almost fifty years ago and was greatly responsible for the commencement operations at Pyramiden and Barentsburg. He made many mining surveys in West Spitsbergen and here in Ny Alesund he has driven the Number Five shaft.'

The deputy inspector of mines paused to blow his nose and consult a piece of paper. 'He came first to Svalbard from a great way across the ocean. Now he comes back on his last survey. He will rest in the northern land he knew so many years ago.'

As if embarrassed by the literary flavour of his closing remarks, the deputy inspector bent down abruptly and picked up a handful of earth. The radio officer nudged me and we dropped our heads. The deputy inspector muttered a short prayer in Norwegian and was about to scatter his earth when he noticed the flag was still on the coffin. The maintenance engineer removed it and restored the little wreath. The earth rattled drily on to the lid. Two miners stepped forward and began to shovel the displaced soil back into the grave. The others stood motionless for a moment then turned and spread out and began to collect up the stones which littered the ground.

'Come on,' said the radio officer. 'Everyone must help.' A stone cairn began to grow over the coffin. At first they were placed reverently. As the coffin became covered some of the men started to toss them on. The deputy inspector lit a small cigar. Bland and the radio officer were deep in conversation. A stone the size of a quarter brick ricocheted off the cairn and struck the Swedish tourist on the ankle. He hopped back on his other foot, pink eyes snapping angrily. I thought I heard a laugh from one of the miners.

When the cairn was nearly waist-high the mourners began to disperse. I caught the radio officer's eye and joined him and

Bland. We walked back together. Randers followed with the inspector.

'I suppose,' I murmured, 'that a body will last for ever in the Arctic.'

'Not like that,' said the radio officer, jerking his head. 'Deeper in the ground, yes. It would be like a refrigerator. There he is too exposed.'

Bland was silent. He walked erectly and purposefully.

I asked, 'Are your quarters ashore comfortable?'

'The beds are wooden planks, Mr Panton. The food is terrible. Frozen potatoes. They are black right through. Old bread, old cheese. A little fish. Tinned milk in the coffee. You would not enjoy it. But we cannot grumble. We are lucky to have anywhere to stay. Ny Alesund is depressed just now, you know. The mines are almost at a standstill. There are only a few people living here. Perhaps our scheme will help bring some new prosperity.'

'That would be very Okay,' said the radio officer. He dropped back to intercept his captain, who was coming up with the Swedish tourist. The latter was limping slightly.

We neared the languishing settlement. The great snow slopes swept up behind the houses. Ice floes winked in the fjord. The conical peaks ringed the scene in every direction, save down the fjord towards the open sea.

I said to Bland, 'It is very beautiful.' I meant it.

'Very beautiful.'

'It must have cast a spell over Mr Williams for him to have wanted his body sent all this way.'

'It is remarkable,' agreed Bland. Wasn't there something he should have queried and hadn't? He added with apparent indifference, 'The wireless officer tells me that you are reporting on the affair for a newspaper. I did not know you were a journalist.'

'Oh, not really.' I managed a self-effacing laugh. Trust the radio officer to gossip. Lucky I hadn't transacted my cables through him. 'I arranged with a friend on a newspaper to send them an article if I came across anything interesting. I'm not a proper journalist, I'm afraid.'

It was rather a different fib from the one I'd told the radio officer. I hoped he hadn't been too detailed in his tale-bearing.

Bland seemed satisfied, however. 'And you will write about Mr Williams?'

Was that the thing that hadn't been quite right? The name Williams. The first time anyone had mentioned it in the present company was when I dropped it casually a moment earlier. Now Bland himself had said it, equally casually. Neither of us had qualified it by adding 'the dead man' or 'the body', or anything like that. Wasn't some sort of reaction to have been expected? 'Ah, you mean the dead man?' Perhaps not.

The question that Bland *had* uttered still quivered in the air. Was I going to write about Williams?

'I doubt it,' I said. 'There is so much I have found that is more interesting.'

'You can tell me?'

'Of course. Things like the coal mining. The Russians, or what little we have seen of them. The American couple who went hunting. The Cambridge expedition. There is much of interest.'

'One would think so,' said Bland.

'The ornithological aspect would also interest my readers,' I said. 'There is much interest in birdlife in Britain now, thanks to television.'

'Indeed. Are you an ornithologist, Mr Panton?'

'No, no. I have merely picked up a little knowledge from a Penguin.'

'I do not understand. There are no penguins in the Arctic, only in the Antarctic.'

'I'm sorry. A Penguin *book* — a small paper-bound book.' I laughed.

There was no answering smile.

'Finally,' I said, 'there is your own splendid scheme, so close in spirit to movements we have in my own country — movements designed to bring out the latent adventure in our youth. I think that is perhaps the most interesting thing of all I shall have to tell my readers.'

Bland stopped. Was that a frown? 'Of course,' he said quietly, 'you are free to write whatever you like. But it is unfortunate that you have not told me earlier that you are also a journalist. Regarding you as a travel agent and as a colleague I have told you things which are really confidential...'

I raised my hand. 'Dr Bland,' I declared, 'I do understand.' It rhymed absurdly. 'I would not dream of taking advantage of your confidences. What aspect of the scheme is it that you would like kept secret?'

'*Secret*? I hardly think we require secrets. It is only that we feel the moment is not right for publicity. After all, there are still negotiations to be completed...'

'Of course there are.'

'When everything is settled, when the time is right, we will welcome publicity. It is perhaps a little early now... Mr Randers will be in charge of our press relations.'

'Say no more,' I said expansively. To my surprise Bland extended his hand. We shook. An Englishman's bond, I told myself.

Ilse was waiting by the gangplank. 'Won't be a minute,' I called.

Outside the saloon Bland said, 'So. We shall knock loudly on your cabin door on Sunday morning, very early.'

'I'll be waiting,' I said.

The radio officer buttonholed me as I was hurrying back to the gangway. Was it news of Dancer?

'Have you heard something?' I asked.

He looked puzzled, then remembered. 'Ah, the friend. No, nothing yet. I was going to tell you something about this Dr Bland we were with. I didn't know you knew him well.'

I looked at my watch. It was after twelve already. Still, it might he important. 'I don't really. Only through Randers. What about him?'

'Oh, just that I knew him in the war.'

'*What*? Where?'

'Here in Norway. At Narvik. He doesn't remember me, I guess. I was just a civilian radio operator in the weather service. But I remember him. He hasn't altered the smallest, except that then he was in uniform. He was a captain in the Kriegsmarine. Lots of gold rings and a wing-collar for church parade. I remember him.'

Suddenly things looked as if they might fall into place. 'Was he — he was a U-boat captain, wasn't he?'

The radio officer spat on the deck and then rubbed out the spit mark with the toe of his brown shoe. 'The Herr Captain Doctor Bland a U-boat captain — that's nice. He was a dry-land sailor. He sat on his ass in an office in Narvik. He was in charge of the weather service. That's how I knew him.'

CHAPTER TWENTY-SIX

For the third time I said, 'Are you sure Maia won't change her mind and come?'

Ilse shook her head. She was beginning to look dispirited. We were striding out on our promised exploration along the fjord. The first part was back the way I had just come, across the green plain, past the new grave, towards the mines — which was mildly frustrating in itself. But nothing compared with Maia's defection. It was a cruel blow.

'This sickness is very sudden,' I grumbled. 'She was perfectly all right last night.'

'You know how it is with girls. She is very sorry.'

'No doubt she is. So am I. I was looking forward to us all going.'

Poor Ilse said nothing.

'I've half a mind to go back,' I said, slowing down 'There's a lot of things I ought to do.' As indeed there were.

'I don't see why it should matter,' said Ilse. 'It is not as if you were Peter…'

'What do you mean?'

'Well, Peter was a little sweet about Maia. He has kissed her goodbye and given her a badge to wear as a souvenir.'

'Oh, he has, has he?' I stopped altogether and looked back. A miniature motorboat was nibbling its way across the fjord like a caterpillar across a leaf. Bland and Co?

Ilse turned, too. 'We'd better go back then.' Her face was flushed and I thought I caught her eyes blinking. I began to feel a bit of a heel.

'No, come on,' I said. 'We might as well go on now.'

We continued in silence. Another little engine and truck chuffed along the railway. The driver gazed incuriously at us. We were walking on dead, dry turf, yellowish green in colour and sprinkled with patches of tiny white and heliotrope flowers. Posts were stuck haphazardly into the ground, sometimes linked by loose strands of wire. A rubbish pit smelled. Further off stood a high flagpole.

The mine workings were deserted except for the sounds of hammering coming from a hut. We passed the entrance to one of the shafts. It was impressive in an unspectacular way. The pithead was only a low structure of brick and wood sloping into the ground; within, the actual tunnel gaped with dramatic candour, a hole to the centre of the earth. On one side were rails for coal trucks. Elsewhere the shaft bottom was trodden clay that shone faintly in the glow of electric lights that receded away to infinity. The banging stopped. A man in dirty overalls came out of the hut, tugging at his flies. When he saw Ilse he changed direction and went behind another building. We moved on. The sluminess soon vanished. A stone hut with a crimson door which I guessed was the explosives store was the last sign of civilization. Now there was only the green-blue fjord, the yellow-green turf, the whiteness of snow and the pale-blue sky above.

We worked our way towards the water's edge and transferred from the turf to a narrow beach of colourless sand and bleached pebbles. With belated consideration I took over from Ilse the haversack containing our lunch. She started to make conversation again. Where had I been before for holidays? Did I like walking? Was there country near London for walking? I answered briefly at first but more cordially as time went on. The sun was in a clear sky and unexpectedly warm. I took my pullover off and Ilse her anorak. The air was invigorating. I couldn't help feeling more amiable.

But after an hour the glacier at the head of the fjord seemed no nearer, while looking back Ny Alesund had shrunk to miniscule size.

'How much further?' I demanded.

Ilse weighed it up. 'Five kilometres,' she suggested.

'*Numpitz!* More like fifteen,' I said. 'It's the air. It's so clear.'

'We have plenty of time.'

'I'm hungry.'

We walked for another forty-five minutes. It was one thirty p.m.

'Far enough,' I said. 'Far enough.'

The glacier actually did look a bit nearer now. It glistened beckoningly. On the other hand the just-perceptible specks which hovered about it were birds, and their minuteness indicated the distance still to go, as well as the scale of the blue ice cliffs.

'They must be twenty or thirty metres high,' I said.

Ilse sat down on a hummock. 'We will have something to eat?'

I unslung the haversack and she began to unpack bread, butter, cheese, some cold meat, two hard-boiled eggs — and a bottle of beer.

'For you,' she said.

I was touched.

'I'll put it in the water to make it cool,' said Ilse. She crossed the little strip of sand and leaned over to stand the bottle in the fjord. Then balancing on one leg she took off a shoe and sock and dipped her foot in.

'Cold?'

'A little.' She came back and stood uncertainly. Her face was glowing and there were dark patches at the armpits of her woollen shirt. 'It would be interesting to swim.'

'It would be cold. *Brrr*!'

'No, not very cold. I tried with my foot.' She wiggled it. The big toe was a little crooked. 'And it would be nice to say one had swum in the Arctic.'

As a matter of fact, the prospect wasn't utterly chilling. The sun was shining from a large acreage of blue sky, which meant it would continue to shine for some time. The fjord shimmered, and close to shore was as clear as spring-water. But the wink of ice floes further out was a useful deterrent.

'No thanks. You go ahead. Anyway, no towel.'

'I brought one.' The grub had been wrapped in a ship's towel. She hesitated, one hand on the zip of her slacks.

I said, 'I'll hide my eyes,' and lay back looking up at the remote blue and wondering what she had in mind. Was this a further ensnarement move? Of course the Finns were well known to be indifferent to nudity. Anyway, she had perhaps brought her costume. There was a splashing and a sharp cry and intake of breath, so I sat up to see. She hadn't, and she was certainly all woman and very nicely so, especially in this particular setting. From the sound effects I deduced she had floundered into the water fast and fiercely, as the brave do. Now she was up again, half facing me, not much more than knee-deep. Against the colour-transparency background she was pink and solid. She laughed unembarrassedly, pushing her wet hair back from her face and raining tiny drops back into the fjord. Her breasts were full but high and well-splayed. Her body was thick but her broad hips made it look all right. The pubic tuft was a dark and equilateral triangle.

She turned and with a thrust from white, strong buttocks fell forward again in a flurry of foam. I wondered whether to go in too, but even as I wondered she completed half a dozen vigorous strokes away from shore, ducked and made the same number back. A moment later she heaved up like Venus in the picture, and the next thing, I was trying to dodge the drops. As she towelled herself, modesty set in to the extent that she turned her back. Close to, the prospect wasn't quite so pleasing. The skin of her haunches, I couldn't help noticing, was rough and goose-pimpled. *Both* big toes were crooked. Her legs were a little too short for her body.

Absent-mindedly I took a slice of bread and cheese and bit a mouthful off, which was hardly tactful if this were to be the big seduction scene. Luckily, it wasn't. Either from lack of encouragement, or the wind whose sharpness I was also beginning to feel, she got dressed. Pants and bra of sensible white stuff, trousers, shirt, socks, shoes, and as an afterthought the anorak. I pulled on my pullover to keep company.

'You should have come in too,' she said, sitting down opposite to me.

'I know. You were too quick. I have to get around to the idea slowly.'

'I hope I did not disturb you. At home we are used to men and women bathing together.'

'Not at all. I thought how fine you looked.'

She was pleased. I felt I could decently take another bite of bread and cheese and go and fetch the beer.

As I sat down again she said, 'What a pity Maia could not come.' Perhaps it was a test remark, to educe my reactions. Well, it would have been something to see *her* skipping about in the altogether. But I was content enough at the moment.

The beer was cold, the food was good. Beyond the glacier three perfect Fujiyama mountains — the Tre Kroner, or Three Crowns, according to the pamphlet — were poised in the clear air. By the water's edge a pair of little seabirds which I couldn't identify shepherded their brood along in careful echelon. The babies were brown and fluffy and tended to lag behind and then spurt forward with frantic wagglings of their tiny rumps.

I said, 'It can't be helped.'

'Colin.'

'Yes.'

'I must tell you something. I have lied. Maia is not sick. She has gone with the Dr Bland and Mr Randers.'

I cracked my hard-boiled egg on a stone. 'Yes. I guessed that's what was happening.'

From somewhere a cloud moved across the sun, and the smile vanished from the landscape.

CHAPTER TWENTY-SEVEN

The trudge back wasn't much fun. For the most part it was conducted in broody silence. As we neared Ny Alesund again I found myself staring more and more fixedly across the fjord. On the far shore some little buildings showed up clearly against the snow. They were the long abandoned installations of an English company which had attempted to quarry marble. New London the settlement had been called, with a touching faith in a future expansion that had never come. Beyond New London, over the hills behind, past Grimaldi peak, dropping down to another inlet of the sea, lay the equally unproductive hectares of the Caledonian Spitsbergen Development Corporation. There the names were bravely Scottish. Holyroodhamna, indeed!

Now the playground of Sparta was to rise there. The peace of the Arctic — the precious, natural *stillness* that I was just beginning to notice properly — would be violated by the shouting and singing of Youth. I could see them already, bare-chested on the seashore, exercising with great logs of bleached driftwood; or setting off into the hills roped together in body and mind; or grouped vocally round the campfires in the dusk. Except, of course, that there wouldn't be any dusk.

Meanwhile there was a vision more dreary and more immediate. At this very instant Holyroodhamna would be echoing to the gruff speech of Bland and Randers — and little Maia. She would be posing for more pictures for the wretched Spartapol prospectus — perhaps in shorts or bathing costume, perhaps in nothing at all, as some kind of spirit or symbol of *Spartapolismus*.

'We had both been asked to go,' said Ilse breaking the silence. 'But the Dr Bland said there was only one bed in Ny Alesund where a girl could properly sleep tonight, in the house of the mine engineer. His wife is the only one left in the town this summer. Besides, I have preferred to stay aboard the steamship.'

I grunted. Ilse's story, which she was sticking to this time, was that Maia had been approached by Bland again, as unexpectedly as before. He had asked her if she would be interested in becoming an instructor when the camp opened. The season would coincide with her school holidays in Finland. Maia had reacted with enthusiasm. Bland had then asked her if she would remain in Ny Alesund while the *Bellsund* went further north, so that she could visit the site and give her advice. There would also be some more pictures. It was all so preposterous that I had to believe it.

'But why that tale about her being sick?' I demanded.

'She was this morning, a little,' said Ilse. 'Also the Dr Bland has said that you might be cross because you cannot go across until Sunday.' I was, now.

At the post office there was a radio message from Rogerson. It was brief and to the point: 'RING ME REVERSE CHARGEring me reverse charge.' The number followed. I booked the call and in the twenty minutes' waiting time took a perfunctory look at the house that Bland had suggested might suit us as a hotel. It didn't seem to matter very much anymore.

Rogerson's voice came and went like an old-fashioned radio report but I heard him well enough.

'I expected you to call earlier,' he began.

'Sorry.'

'Never mind. It means I've been held up this end, that's all. When are you going to the Krossfjorden site?'

'Day after tomorrow.' I explained Bland's proposal.

'Not much good. Now, you're staying aboard the *Bellsund* for the last part of the trip?'

'Yes, I suppose so.'

'Do you know where you'll be tomorrow?'

Luckily I had the ship's brochure in front of me, crumpled but open at the right place. 'Magdalena Bay a.m., Danish Island p.m., it says in the leaflet.'

'All right. I'll get on to a man called Tarn. He runs a hunting ketch called the *Harriet*.'

'I've seen it.'

'If I can get him, he'll pick you up at one of those places. If he can't do it I'll have to think of something else. Is it safe to reach you aboard ship?'

'The radio officer's an awful old gossip but it should be all right now Bland and Co. have gone off.' I heard myself replying prosaically while my private thoughts went reeling off into disbelief. This wasn't happening to *me*.

'Right. Now listen carefully. Here's the plan.'

I listened with the same spurious detachment. At the end he said, 'All clear now?'

'Yes, I think so. There's a couple of other things I wanted to ask you, though. One is, have you heard anything about an Englishman called Dancer? He had a cabin on the coastal steamer that I should have had if I hadn't come to see you…'

'Well?' lie sounded impatient.

'He seems to have disappeared, that's all. I wondered if…'

'I'll see what I can pick up. What else?'

'It's about Bland. Something the radio man told me. Do you know if the Germans had weather stations in Spitsbergen in the War?'

'Yes, of course.'

'Where exactly?'

'Don't know offhand. Could find out and radio them. Why?'

'Just a hunch. By the way, did you know the late Williams?'

'I did.' The voice was grim.

I said, 'Do we get any pips or anything?'

'No. But I'm ringing off now. Good luck.'

'Thank you.' He'd already gone, though.

CHAPTER TWENTY-EIGHT

IT was midnight and the *Bellsund* was heading gingerly north again on the last stage of her journey: the touristic excursion, conditions permitting, to Magdalena Bay, Danish Island and points north; to a possible glimpse of pack ice; to within a mile or two of the eightieth parallel. Outside, a white wet mist hid the coastline. The midnight sun filtered its light through an unbroken helmet of cloud. Sea and sky were uniformly opaque. Silence was complete. It was like being inside a bubble.

I lay on my bunk. It was the first time I had had the cabin to myself. Ilse, I reflected, and not for the first time, would also be on her own. At dinner she had appeared shyly to eat in the first-class saloon. The radio officer, sponsoring her, had explained, 'We cannot have her eating all on her own now that her friend is ashore.'

I'd jumped up and made her sit opposite me, and gone on to be as amiable as possible: to try and make up for the afternoon. We'd even had a game of draughts afterwards; I won. I looked down again at the radio message which had arrived from Rogerson two hours previously. The radio officer, eyes popping with curiosity, had brought it to me in person. He'd printed out the text in blue crayon capitals: 'WEATHER STATIONS UNTIL 1945 AT STORMBUKTA RIJPFD HOPEN LIEFDEFD ADVENTFD KROSSFD STOP NO DANCING NEWS.'

The last bit was an unlikely joke to come from Rogerson. I decided it must have been a communications mistake and studied the names. Krossfjorden was the one that mattered, of course.

I hadn't expected my guesswork to be backed up quite so precisely. It would have been helpful to know that there had been a weather station near Krossfjorden. To find that there had been one actually sited there was indeed a bull's-eye.

According to the little map that came with the handout pamphlet, Krossfjorden was longer and slightly narrower than Kingsbay, and ran into the sea immediately north of it. I'd looked out when we passed by about dinner time, but there was only mist and crumbling cliffs and wheeling seabirds to be seen. On the map the two fjords met at right angles, like the arms of a capital 'L'. They were separated by the triangular wedge of land which contained somewhere the answer to the whole mystery.

Where exactly? Bland had named Holyroodhamna as his site, placing a precise finger on the south side of Krossfjorden, about half-way up its length. The little map didn't go to such details. It didn't matter at the moment. Wait a minute — didn't I have something else? I fumbled among the dirty socks and handkerchiefs accumulating at the bottom of my grip. Somewhere there should be the cutting I had pinched from the *Scotsman* office.

With a pang of guilt I discovered it crumpled and torn. I smoothed it out. There again was all the sober optimism of the Caledonian Spitsbergen Development Corporation complete with picture of Harry Williams and a little sketch-map. And yes — the map showed Holyroodhamna. Alongside the name was a symbol that stood for Iron. I looked down the text.

Holyroodhamna, it said, was the site of one of the Corporation's most ambitious projects — reported to be a rich and extensive vein of haematite or brown iron ore … a drift mine had been driven and worked for eighteen months … in 1931 a total of 2,100 tons shipped away.

There must have been jovial scenes at the next annual general meeting of the Caledonian Spitsbergen Corporation, actually getting something out of the place. Then — the usual story — operations discontinued as uneconomical in 1932.

I fetched a glass of water from the washbasin. The bottle of Longyear beer was still on the floor below. It was pleasing to have things fit together, like solving a tricky motivation problem in a script (not that *Simon de Montfort* had needed much motivation). I had an overwhelming conviction that the wartime weather station in Krossfjorden had something to do with the decision to build Spartapol there. If the camp site proved to be hard by the weather station it would be decisive. But what was the motive, the connection? This was where a flashback would have been useful. You can have them in the movies whenever you want. It's harder in real life.

I closed my eyes and tried to picture the fjord. I made it like any other Spitsbergen fjord, only narrower, as the map suggested. It was 1945, in the spring. The first exquisitely-hued days of lightness had broken the long Polar night. In the foreground was a hut, and by it a tall mast. From the hut men came running. They stopped and shielded their eyes as they looked down the fjord. It had been perhaps seven months since they'd had any contact with the outside world other than by radio. Was this the supply boat at last, bringing fresh food, letters from the homeland, long-delayed Christmas cards, even the chance of leave? Or was it the dark shape of a U-boat on some secret errand from beleaguered Germany…?

Well, it could be anything I cared to make it, and there were plenty more clichés as trusty as the U-boat one waiting to be slotted in. I hadn't been a twice-a-week film-goer since thirteen for nothing. But the odd thing was that I had some intuition that I was on the right track, and that it was bound up with

Bland. Even if he hadn't been a U-boat captain he'd been in the German Navy, and he'd been in charge of the weather service for this part of the world.

I closed my eyes. Sleep was far away. I opened my eyes. The cabin was full of dead light that cast no shadows yet left everything in shadow. It was neither light nor dark, neither hot nor cold. I pulled the feather bed over me and then pushed it off. It made no difference. I got up and pulled on my slacks over my pyjamas. I had no slippers, so I had to put on shoes and socks. Finally the pullover. I picked up the big bottle of beer and collected both tooth-glasses, Randers's and mine. There was something else. I found them in my grip, opened the cabin door and slipped out.

Use said softly, 'Who is it?' She probably hadn't been asleep.

'Only me,' I said. I closed the door behind me. A quick look to make sure the other bunk — Maia's bunk — was empty. It was reproachful in its virgin whiteness. 'I couldn't sleep. Hope you don't mind.'

It was a pretty wet thing to say, but I couldn't think of an alternative. You have to say *something*. What was Casanova's opening gambit when he sneaked in off the balcony?

'No. Come in.' She switched on her headlight and sat up. I can't say she looked displeased.

I wondered whether to sit on the foot of her bunk or on the empty one. I settled for the former, put the beer on the ground and produced the glasses.

'I thought we might have a quiet little party,' I suggested. Ilse beamed. She could see through the niceties, that one. She sat up. She was wearing striped pyjamas, like a man's. I unscrewed the beer and poured her a glass. The other one was smeared with toothpaste.

'Fetch mine from the washbasin,' said Ilse.

I stood up.

Clunk! It was one of those terrible blows right on the top of the head, mathematically in the middle, the sort that drive your head half-way down into your body, rattle your back teeth and leave a brief but unendurable pain. I gave a cautious shriek of despair and sat down again. It was the upper bunk. After lording it in the first class I'd forgotten about upper bunks. At least it provided the next ploy. Ilse's anticipatory leer vanished comically. Her eyes clouded with concern. 'You hurt yourself?' she cried, leaning forward.

'Cruelly,' I said. I felt my head apprehensively. Could a bump like that affect the thin spot on top? It certainly wouldn't do it any good.

Isle scrambled forward on her knees and examined the place, then planted a moist kiss on it. Inside the pyjama jacket her breasts nudged my face. It seemed only fair to give them a kiss in return.

'Poor Colin,' she cooed. 'Poor man.'

'I know,' I said. 'Poor man.' I needed a beer. This time I straightened up more circumspectly and made it. After I'd had a gulp it wasn't difficult to resume a position of some chumminess. To be exact, we were now on the same bunk and facing the same way and I had my arm about Ilse's shoulders. She snuggled up. From this angle she was really quite pretty: her face more pointed and feminine, her bare arms softer and rounder in the electric light. I set my glass down carefully and began to undo her pyjama buttons.

She watched the operation gravely, then leaned forward to assist the removal of the jacket. I moved my hand down. They *were* man's pyjamas. I tugged the cord and the knot loosened.

'*Du, du, du.*' It was a marvellous sort of gurgle of satisfaction at the turn events had taken.

I lay back a moment and felt for the bottle. Not for a drink but to make sure that it stood in a safe place. Ilse propped herself on an elbow and looked down on me. Her eyes were suddenly dark. Her hand was inside my pyjama jacket rubbing my chest. She rubbed very hard and the hand was rough but the sensation was fine. I reached up and hauled her down. She was tremendously solid and she smelled of new mown hay. Presently, in the grey twilight, we came to our separate satisfactions. It was like two trains rushing past each other in the night, when for a moment you see into lighted compartments and then they're gone again with only a picture of a man with a glass to his lips left fleetingly fixed on the retina.

Afterwards the old dog came padding along that follows every loveless love-making, the one called Dismay. I rolled aside and found a cigarette, feeling shabby. The pale shape of Maia's bunk was additional reproach. It was too easy for the man. It was taking all and giving nothing in return, except the moment. For the girl it was something more. She offered her body in exchange for a bit of your real you, to buy some claim to you, some affection. And poor old Ilse, I thought as I stroked her hair, you haven't a hope.

Reaction to reaction: she'd asked for it clearly enough and, now she'd had it, seemed highly satisfied. I aimed a kick at Dismay, who slunk away. When her breathing became regular I put one foot down cautiously, and two minutes later the second. A careful transference of weight and I was upright.

I stood for another minute, then went over to the washbasin and splashed a little water about. The breathing carried on.

I edged along to Maia's bunk and perched on the end, puffing a cigarette as camouflage and keeping my eyes on Ilse all the time. Very carefully I let my hand drop into the blue valise and stir around. I identified a little blouse, the fluffy cotton sweater, a pair of slippers and one of those cardboard boxes that seem to be the same size and shape the world over. I pushed it aside quickly. A little brassiere I let linger in my hand a moment.

I delved deeper. At the bottom were shoes, a couple of books, an apple, a roll of film, a brush, and finally the thing I sought: Maia's journal, the thick elastic band around its middle identifying it. I drew it out and carefully inched the band off. Released from tension it shot away from my fingers, somewhere into the dark. I swore softly and felt for it. The opposite bunk creaked and Ilse stirred. I froze until her breathing grew regular again. The band turned up under the washbasin.

There was hardly enough light to read Maia's cramped hand even had I been able to understand the language. I leafed through the book vaguely hoping for some sign, though of what I really didn't know. Some photograph or document stored between the pages, maybe, that would make everything clear.

'What are you doing?' Ilse's eyes were open and watchful. I slipped the elastic band back over the diary and dropped it into the valise, stubbed the cigarette with a hiss into the washbasin, padded back to her. All right, she should know. I wanted her to know.

'I don't understand Maia,' I said simply. 'It troubles me. I don't like these people, I don't like this camp. Why should she leave you and go with them for two days just because they ask her? It doesn't make sense. I thought she must have other reasons, like not being a Finnish girl at all, or being related to someone…'

Ilse sat up, reaching behind her to prop up a pillow with a movement that showed off her really very serviceable breasts.

'I would like a drink of beer,' she said.

'Of course. Sorry.'

She sipped it. She said slowly, 'I am the German one, not Maia. My father was German soldier, my mother is Finnish. But it is nothing to do with such things.' She sighed. 'I think you do not understand about where we live. Rovaniemi is a very far north town, a long way even from Helsinki. Maia has only twice been out of Finland and never out of Scandinavia. At home she is a pretty girl but not very bright — you understand? Her father is a workman and she is just a physical teacher at a children's school. There is not much money.'

I poured the last of the beer for myself. 'Go on.'

'Well, this camp has sounded wonderful to her. She thinks she will be meeting people from all the other countries and that she will always be doing what she is best at — the games and sports. It will be like … it will be like the year we have had the Olympic Games in Helsinki, only it will be every year.'

'Is that all?'

'Yes. I believe so.'

'There is no other attraction?'

'There is no need. The one is enough.'

'I suppose you're right.' I wasn't very conclusive but I felt a lightening of the spirits. Any rationalization of the Spartapol appeal was better than none.

I took off all my things — well, almost all — and climbed in beside her. The bunk was narrow. This time I wanted it to be better. I wanted to love her, to be nice to her, to *value* her. I wanted to give as well as receive; and in time that's what happened.

'Why do you keep on your socks?' she said sleepily at last.

I looked down at my feet. I'd never thought. 'I dunno,' I said. 'Just do, that's all.'

CHAPTER TWENTY-NINE

Next morning we went ashore in a conducted party in Magdalena Bay. It was one of the tourist things to do. They rigged a stepladder affair down the side of the *Bellsund* and launched a motor cutter. The handful of us who were left aboard scrambled inexpertly down the one and into the other.

The captain, somewhat surprisingly, came too, huddled inside the turned up collar of his greatcoat. It was cold and dank. I shivered. Ilse looked at me with concern. She had a proprietorial air this morning that was a bit alarming. But she looked pretty enough with the hood of her anorak turned up, and somehow smaller. I felt correspondingly more protective.

The bay was narrower than any of the others we'd ventured into. There was much more of the sense of being in a land-locked stretch of water. The inevitable black-streaked mountains crowded in from every direction. Two or three glaciers terminated in frozen waterfalls poised over the still surface.

The cutter burbled blue smoke and oily bubbles and set off with us up the inlet. The mist was thinning and a faint ray of sunlight poked through the clouds. There was much production of cameras and aiming of exposure meters and setting of shutters. A greenish-blue ice floe the size of a grand piano slid by. The cameras clicked. The floe bobbed up and down in the boat's wake.

The captain, sitting stiffly in the stern, raised an arm and pointed to a flurry in the water and a glimpse of a glossy black head. Cameras were raised and lowered again in frustration. The seal was too far off.

I looked back anxiously at the *Bellsund*, already dwindling into a miniature ship. Surely the ketch wouldn't come so soon … if it did, it might miss me.

'What is the matter?' said Ilse.

'Nothing.'

We approached within fifty yards of the biggest glacier, towering up at this range like a cliff and seeming to radiate coldness. I shivered again, and wished I had warmer clothes. Eighty north, and not even an overcoat. The cutter chugged round in a lazy semicircle and headed across the fjord towards a rocky shore. The captain stood up to direct the helmsman and the boat nudged in. One at a time we scrambled ashore. I got my left foot submerged somehow and even a ski-boot won't keep out sea-water. I cursed.

Ilse said again, 'What is the matter?'

'I got my foot wet.'

We milled around on the slippery barren shore for a long twenty minutes. There wasn't even the sick turf of Ny Alesund here. Only rocks and water, and, the minute you started to clamber up from sea-level, snow. The sun had disappeared again.

Lunch as the *Bellsund* forged on, pony-tail of black smoke streaming behind and seabirds planing or beating alongside, according to species. I talked desultorily with Ilse and kept a watch through the saloon windows. What if the *Harriet* hove in sight now? What would happen then? I wondered just how powerful Rogerson was.

We reached Danish Island at two thirty, and still no sign of the ketch. This was the last opportunity for a convenient rendezvous. I decided not to say anything to Ilse unless they did turn up. Secretly I was beginning to hope they didn't. It had sounded a neat idea when Rogerson propounded it over the radio-telephone. In these high, inhospitable latitudes it was fast losing its charm.

The sun had disappeared again, and, further out at sea now, the wind was keener. I had a brain-wave and unpacked the plastic mac from the little pouch where it had nestled ever since I bought it. It was pale and flimsy and urban but at least it kept out the wind. We went ashore to a strange rocky plain littered with debris. There were splintered baulks of timber, mounds of red-rusted iron shavings, great chunks of broken earthenware. We wandered off into ones and twos, silent, marvelling.

'What happened?' said Ilse.

I'd read about it in the pamphlet. 'A man called André, a Swede, set off from here to sail across the North Pole to America in a balloon. Two others went with him. They made gas for the balloon by pouring acid on iron. This was the iron.' I picked up a handful. 'The acid came in these pots.' I kicked a thick fragment. It was glazed brown on the outside, still cleanly pale on the inside, untouched by time or weather.

'What became of them?'

'No one knew for thirty years. Then someone found their bodies and all their gear on White Island. That's towards Russia. The wind blew the wrong way. The cold had preserved everything intact. You know, the people as well.'

Ilse shivered.

'It was a long time ago,' I said. 'Sixty years.'

'Why did they do it?'

'Why does anyone try and do anything?'

'I don't understand.'

'Sometimes,' I said, 'you have to do things. You get an idea which is so big or so wild or so stupid that you can't leave it alone. So you have to do something about it.'

'I see.' Dubiously.

'With people like me,' I added judicially, 'it doesn't happen very often. About once in five hundred years.'

I powdered the iron in my hand and let it trickle away, trying to picture the scene as it must have looked at the time. Two or three buildings. Neat stacks of stores. Ranks of brown jars. Men scurrying around like ants. A dinghy ferrying final supplies from the stubby sealer anchored off-shore. Andre, bearded, impatient to be off. The gas-bag slowly swelling. Sharp smell of acid biting on iron. All to end in a whimsical drift in the wrong direction, descent on a barren island high on the crown of the world, and the slow death of hope.

'People fly over the Pole every day now,' I said. 'In DC-7s, knocking back Martinis and eating chicken.'

It was Ilse who first spotted the *Harriet*. 'The Americans!' she cried.

I jerked round. The slim white shape was gliding into anchorage alongside the shabby *Bellsund*. I nerved myself for the plunge.

'Ilse, I've got something to tell you.'

'Yes?'

It was a curious reversal of the situation on the shore at Ny Alesund twenty-four hours — was that all? — before.

'I think I'm going with the Americans for a day. Or on their boat, anyway.' I'd considered excuses but rejected them all. Invitation from the Rennicks to join them. A likely story! Cable from London requesting article about hunting. That was hardly better.

162

She said, 'Where will you go?'

'I'm not sure yet. It's something I've got to do, really. Otherwise this whole journey would have been a waste of time.' I had this compulsion to be honest with the girl.

'I understand.'

'I'll rejoin you all tomorrow at Ny Alesund.'

'That will be good.'

Oh, the obedient acceptance! If she had done anything it would have been preferable. But she just took it.

I went back to the *Bellsund* with the rest of the party, collected a spare pair of socks and an extra packet of cigarettes, said suitable things to the radio officer first and then to the captain, and waited for the small boat from the *Harriet* to come over and collect me.

It came in due course, manned by a single seaman. Ilse had vanished. I guessed where she might be and clattered up to the little day-cabin

'See you tomorrow evening,' I said. What else could I?

'Colin?'

'What?'

'Be careful.'

I kissed her goodbye.

CHAPTER THIRTY

I descended the ship's ladder for the third time that day, and from the bobbing dinghy a minute later watched it being hauled in. The *Bellsund* would venture a few more miles north and then turn south for Ny Alesund again, arriving there in the small hours of the next morning, Sunday. Everything now depended on timing.

Tarn, the skipper of the *Harriet*, was predictably tough, the kind of Harry Morgan character who might have been designed to go with the fittings on a rich man's hunting ketch. He had stumpy brown teeth, a tanned face, eyes the exact grey of the Arctic Ocean.

'Bill Rogerson is one hell of a man,' he said in English by way of introduction. 'What's all this about?'

'Maybe nothing very much. Didn't he tell you anything?'

'Did he hell! Anyway we'll get going and talk afterwards. Anyone who knows Bill Rogerson is okay by me. I knew him in the war.' He shouted orders in Norwegian.

I heard the Rennicks' voices floating up from somewhere below.

'Sure you don't want to go ashore, honey?' he was saying.

'What would I want that for? There's only a lot of goddam junk there where some nut took off in a balloon.'

'What did you tell them?' I asked Tarn with a nod below. The *Harriet* was already driving south to the throb of diesel.

'Well, I couldn't tell 'em much. I just said it was an emergency call and that was that. They were mad all right. I had to offer to suspend the charter fee for the hunting time they lose.' Like anyone in the tourist business he knew the right business words.

'I'm awfully sorry about that. It'll only be a day, I promise.' But that was fifty quid.

'That's okay. I told 'em it was to do with the Secret Service and the Soviets. It was Bill's idea. He told me.'

'I bet they didn't like that.'

'They didn't. But it stopped the beefing. It was the woman, not the man. He was okay. They'd had one day in Liefdefjorden without smelling a bear. I was going to take 'em on to Nordauslandet today. You want a rest or anything?'

'Don't think so. What time do we get there?'

'Well, off Cape Mitra in two, two and a half hours. Can't go much further than that without the chance of being sighted from Krossfjorden. Depends on visibility.'

'It was misty yesterday.'

'Uh-huh. We'll see.'

'I don't need a rest, anyway, thanks.'

'We'll fix you something to eat before you go. Dinner below ain't until seven thirty.'

It was now four thirty. That meant Cape Mitra about seven p.m. Allow another two hours, maybe three, that would be nine p.m. at the earliest before I would reach the old weather station; about right, and quite safe.

I'd told Tarn pretty well everything I could. He'd listened carefully, only asking one or two shrewd questions and occasionally correcting a placename. He even knew the exact site of the weather station, which was a positive aid. Whether he believed any of it, was hard to determine.

A white-jacketed steward brought a tray of tea into the cockpit.

'English custom,' said Tarn, grinning.

The tray was silver and the tea service Rosenthal china. The tea itself might have come from Fortnums.

'You seem to be doing all right,' I said.

He shrugged. 'Okay.'

'Mostly Americans?'

'Mostly. They're all right. We had Hemingway reserve last year, but he cancelled again. One thing's for sure — they're about the only people got enough money to pay for all this.' His gaze swept over the *Harriet's* gleaming woodwork, polished brass, hooded instrument panel, and finally lit on the Rosenthal china. 'I had one Swedish party last year and one Belgian. This year there's some West Germans coming — they're getting nice and rich, God damn them.'

'No Englishmen ever?'

'Only Bill Rogerson one time, with some Lord Somebody. But Bill was my guest. Yo, that was one hell of a trip. We had a lot of fun. Bill brought a case of Scotch along that was the real stuff. But it's Americans I need. You know how many trips I can get in? Seven a year. That's all. June to September. I just have to charge a lot.'

'I heard you guarantee a Polar bear, though?'

'Yea, that's all they come for. These sort of people, anyway. The scenery or the place don't mean anything. They got to have a bear. Take the skin home. Have themselves photographed with the kill. These two even brought a cinema photographer, would you believe it?'

'I know. I suppose they must be loaded. The funny thing is that old Rennick told me he worked in a bank, that's all.'

'Sure he works in a bank. *His* bank.' He took a gulp of tea. 'The barrier ice is a long way north this year. Did they tell you aboard the *Bellsund*? The tourists won't even sniff it. Means I can get right round the top of the islands now. Used to be solid ice all year. If things don't change again I'll be able to fit in an extra trip, maybe two trips, eh?' He rubbed thumb and forefinger together in the gesture which the world over spells money.

He passed me a small cigar and lit one himself. 'If you've had enough tea, I guess you ought to pay a call on the customers. They're still a little restless about this business, if you get it.'

'Of course,' I said, not very enthusiastically. It promised to be a sticky meeting. Aboard the *Bellsund* we'd hardly exchanged a word. Now I'd commandeered their boat.

'Why, how d'ya do?' said the old man courteously.

'Hi,' said Mrs Rennick. She didn't look over-friendly.

The cabin was small but sumptuous. I wasn't in any mood for making inventories, but the general effect of copper and ebonized beech and blue and white upholstery was enough to be going on with.

I said, 'I'm sorry about all this. You must be very mystified.'

'It is true to say we don't altogether understand the, er, precise nature of your mission,' said Rennick. In the mildly formal atmosphere of the interview he had dropped readily into the American style of slow motion exposition that sounds as if it's being unwound from a coil of barbed wire. 'But if as Captain Tarn says it is of a security nature, then we are, er, naturally ready to be of any assistance we, er, can.'

'Yeah, if,' said Mrs Rennick. They were sitting side by side on a built-in couch which ran the whole of one side of the compartment.

Rennick ignored her and continued to unwind. 'Subject, that is, to the fact that we are United States citizens and would, er, rather not be drawn into any troublesome situation without reference to a, er, United States consular representative.'

'Wherever *he* may be,' snapped Mrs Rennick. 'There isn't one a thousand miles from here, I'll give you.'

'That's very understanding of you, sir,' I said. 'I don't think you need worry about being involved. Anyway, it isn't anything very desperate, really.'

Rennick said, 'Aboard ship I, er, recall you said something about being a screen writer, Mr Prontor.'

Ma chimed in, 'I heard you were in the travel business.'

'Well,' I said, 'I am a screen writer. At least I shared a credit on one picture and wrote another alone that never got made. Also I am doing an errand for a friend in the travel business.'

'What did I tell you?' jeered Mrs Rennick. 'We're being taken for a ride, that's all.'

'No, honestly — I'm not looking for a picture just now, whatever I may have said. Nor is it only a travel business thing, though that does come into it.' I wasn't handling the conversation very well.

Rennick looked at me patiently. He said, 'We came five thousand miles to make this trip, Mr Prontor. It may seem absurd to you, even, er, ridiculous. I know well that I was the object of, er, considerable amusement aboard ship. I don't care. This is what I want and what I worked for all my life. I wasn't in a position to afford the, er, necessary leisure until I was sixty-two, Mr Prontor. That year I went to Alaska. I have since been to East Africa, Assam and some of the Central American states. In all, er, actuarial probability this is my last trip. I would, er, like to make the most of it.'

Ma Rennick reached out and took his hand. I was touched and embarrassed and filled with a sense of futility. My elaborate errand reduced to a foolish imposition on others. I hunted for words.

I said, 'The whole thing I'm doing may be a complete waste of everyone's time. I don't know. I hope not. I can only ask you to believe that the possibility exists that it may be worthwhile.' Rennick nodded. 'I'm no secret agent. I'm what I said. It just happens that I got involved … now I must at least hand it over to someone else.'

The old watery eyes were surprisingly alert. 'That's good enough for me,' said Rennick finally. 'You see' — he turned to his wife — 'this is the way the English do things. They don't specialize the way we do. It doesn't alter the fact that Mr Prontor here is on security work and we cannot complain just because we lose one day — two days' — hunting.'

'Okay, okay.' She gave a reluctant assent. 'Anyway, we hadn't caughten a sight of one lousy polar bear.'

'We weren't in the area for polar bears yet. How many times have I got to tell you? Captain Tarn said we wouldn't be in the area until tonight. Now it will be tomorrow night or even later.'

'It's very kind of you both to be so amenable,' I put in hurriedly. 'I am sure the authorities will be most grateful.'

'You're welcome,' said Ma. She gave a philosophic laugh. 'As long as I get me a polar bear sometime this trip that's all *I* want.'

CHAPTER THIRTY-ONE

The *Harriet* was sliding past one vast glacier after another. There were seven in a row, said Tarn. An hour to go. I began to get a sinking feeling. This was a nice little island of security. I was in no hurry to leave it.

Tarn said, 'Have you got a gun?'

'No.' The idea hadn't crossed my mind.

'You ought to have one.'

'Maybe,' I said doubtfully.

'I got plenty of rifles. But they're no good. There ought to be a revolver somewhere.' He rummaged in a locker and produced a heavy Luger, the great big one with buttons on the block like door-knobs.

'My God, it'd break my arm.'

'Yeah. Anyway I got no goddam ammunition for it.'

He rummaged further. A steel shackle, an old glove, a torch, came to light. If only I'd thought about the torch… Finally Tarn hooked out another pistol. It was even bigger, with a bore of a cool inch.

'A signal pistol,' he said. 'No good.'

'I don't know. Might be just the thing. I don't want to shoot anyone, but I might want to attract their attention.'

'Okay. I'll see if there are any shells.'

He found three in a box: big red fellows like shotgun cartridges. I tried the pistol in my pocket. It felt like a flat-iron, and the butt stuck out a couple of inches.

At six thirty the chef, in a tall white hat, came up with a bowl of soup for me, plus ham sandwiches, cheese and coffee. He stood at the open back of the cockpit, sniffing in the air. Tarn asked him something in Norwegian and listened approvingly to the answer.

He smiled at me and said, 'They got soup tonight, sea-trout, roast ptarmigan, ice-cream, coffee.'

I said, 'Sure. You expect to rough it if you want to go hunting. Did you shoot the ptarmigan yourself?'

'Hell, no. It's out the deep freeze.'

We checked through the arrangements again. The plan was that at Cape Mitra — or a few miles on into the fjord if Tarn guessed it was safe — I was to transfer to the dinghy, powered by an outboard motor and piloted by one of Tarn's two crewmen. The dinghy would hug the north side of the fjord and with reasonable luck would be invisible from the south shore. It would go in at least ten kilometres before turning to cross the fjord. It would land me on the south side beyond the weather station and the old mine, and would then wait for two hours. If I didn't signal with the pistol before the two hours were up it would return the same way. The *Harriet* would start back for the hunting grounds without further delay. If I did signal, the dinghy would follow the shore line until it saw me, and pick me up. In this contingency the *Harriet* would have to forfeit another four hours or so and land me at Ny Alesund.

We arranged a help signal for direst emergencies only. Tarn was reluctant to have his man involved more than necessary.

'But if you're in a spot,' he said, 'fire three. Fire everything. He'll use his judgment.'

It all seemed fairly foolproof.

Cape Mitra loomed up on the port bow. Tarn throttled back his engine and steered in close to the cliffs as the swell of the open sea gradually gave way to smoother water. There was a light mist, but visibility wasn't too poor. Across the mouth of the fjord Grimaldi peak stood out quite plainly.

'I'll chance another three miles,' said Tarn. 'Now then, is there anything else you need?'

'I don't think so.' Why didn't I think of the torch?

'How about clothes?'

'I'm all right. This thing keeps out the cold quite well.' I flicked the plastic mac. 'Anyway, it's only for twelve hours at the most.'

Tarn looked at his watch. 'Cocktail time below,' he said gravely. 'Dry Martinis, Captain, and we like 'em *dry*.' From the galley wafted delicious smells. Sizzling butter. Fish. A roasting smell. I wondered how ptarmigan ptasted.

The *Harriet* crept on. The cliffs were very close now, alive with myriads of seabirds. The Rennicks' cameraman came aloft and began to take readings with his meter.

A splash from the anchor, and the diesel throb subsided. The crewmen set about launching the dinghy. I would have liked to visit the lavatory but felt self-conscious. The Rennicks came up. The cockpit was crowded now. Tarn looked displeased. Old man Rennick had on his big check lumber-jacket and peaked cap. The old head in front of his body veered round like a tortoise's.

He said, 'It's a cold night if you can call it night, Mr Prontor. We guessed you might appreciate this.'

I goggled. 'This' was a long hip-flask, prohibition style, nicely done in stainless steel and calf.

'I can't take that,' I said.

'Course you can. Plenty more like that one. It's got Scotch in it. Come in handy.'

I thanked him, suddenly but acutely aware that the ceremony was being recorded by the cameraman. If I could put the signal

172

shells somewhere else the flask would fit one trouser pocket about as neatly as the pistol fitted the other. I put the shells on the cockpit ledge and tried. At least I was balanced now.

Ma Rennick called, 'Good luck, Mac.'

Tarn said, 'Okay, see you. Give my regards to that old Bill Rogerson.'

I climbed down into the bobbing dinghy as nonchalantly as I could. The cameraman took it. I wished he'd stop. The crew man started the motor, which was only a pipsqueak one, and shoved off. Everyone waved. The last sound I heard above the popple of the outboard was the dinner gong.

It was cold, the dinghy ride. I sat in the bow with my back to the way we were going and snapped all the snap fasteners I could find on the plastic mac. I wished I had a hat. The crewman, whose name wasn't Nils or Lars or anything Nordic, but simply Joe, sat rigidly at the control stick, staring out past my left ear. For a change he would sometimes look past the right one instead. He seemed to be keeping the pipsqueak motor at peak revs. Maybe he was in a hurry to get back. It sounded like an angry scooter and the little prow beneath me was riding high out of the water. The only trouble was that the noise was rather worrying — not so much for itself as for the effect it had on the birds in the cliffs that towered up to port.

They didn't take much notice while we were level. But as we got about twenty yards past a great commotion broke out, with much shouting and beating of wings and taking to the air in fright. I did some inference work and deduced that at a particular angle to our line of progress, say about 110 degrees, the exhaust note was especially sharp. Anyway, the effect was alarming. Krossfjorden wasn't more than three or four miles wide at this point and we would presently be opposite Holyroodhamna. There was enough low mist to shroud our progress otherwise. I made down-beat signs to Joe and with some reluctance he slowed down. The agitation wave diminished appreciably. A fresh anxiety came from the floating ice which thudded against the side of the dinghy.

At the slower speed it was over an hour before Joe pulled the stick over and turned across the fjord. To give him his due he hadn't skimped on the detour so far. Less than a mile further on a narrow spike of land rose from the water. I knew from the map that this was the point where the fjord divided into two arms. It meant that we were well upstream of the mine.

The crossing took about twenty minutes. The clatter of floating ice against the hull was persistent now and still worrying to my unaccustomed ears. Once a large floe gave us a nasty bump, and another time the propeller touched ice with a shrill exclamation.

Joe turned down-fjord as we neared the shore and squinted ahead again over my right shoulder. Any minute now he would be looking for a landing place. On Tarn's chart Holyroodhamna stood in the lee, i.e. on the seaward side, of a headland which the Caledonian surveyors had called Fifeneset. The idea was that I should go ashore on the other side of this headland. It would mean a hike but it gave absolute cover to the operation. I swivelled round and looked, too. A bulge of rock and snow was already looming up. It wasn't exactly a welcoming prospect, least of all at — I checked my watch — at 9.07 p.m. on what promised to be an even longer night than the one on the coastal steamer.

How long ago was that? Just six days. One-four-four hours. Incredible. A week ago I had been in Oslo. Only yesterday Ilse had been disporting in her nothings on the seashore. The marvel worked the other way, of course, if more ominously. Out at sea somewhere was the *Bellsund*, heading back for Ny

Alesund. She would be there in six hours. Three-sixty minutes. In eight hours at the most the absence of C. Panton would be well and truly rumbled. In less than twenty-four hours she'd be on her way again, bound for Longyear and the temperate latitudes. Would C. Panton be aboard?

I think I was pretty sure I would be. People usually are. The faith that nothing will happen to *you* beats strongly in your breast. I wasn't in the least looking forward to what might come, but I doubted if it would be anything more than discomfort and boredom. The coastal-steamer-type willies were absent, so was all indecision. The thing had been irrevocably set up that boozy morning in the miners' canteen at Longyear.

Joe closed down the motor. The dinghy's bow dropped. A minute later we grounded softly on a shingle beach. Joe was out first, pushing past me. I got ashore dry. It was 9.13. I gave him a swig from the Rennicks' flask and took one myself. We compared watches and Joe held up two fingers to remind me he would wait two hours. He never said a word. I don't think he spoke any English. I smiled. He smiled. I left him urinating into the fjord.

CHAPTER THIRTY-TWO

Oh dear, that trudge! By the time I'd gone a quarter of a mile, ice and snow filled my shoes and the wet seeped inexorably up the legs of my trousers. As I toiled, the sleeves of my plastic mac wriggled back from some malignant frictional cause until my wrists were raw and frozen. Twice I sat down, luckily on soft stuff. I think the only thing that kept me going was the thought that if I did give up, the hardship I had already suffered would have been pointless. With every yard of progress the backlog of hardship increased and the need to justify it grew correspondingly fiercer.

The cliffs of the headland were presumably sheer. I didn't know for sure, I hadn't seen them. But I hadn't seriously considered trying to skirt round the thing at water-level. Humping over its neck seemed the only feasible approach, and would have the additional advantage of bringing me on to the scene at Holyroodhamna from the least predictable direction. Which said, the climb up the back of that pile of snow and ice was even worse than the initial stage on the level. To a mountaineer it would have been a trivial slope. I panted and puffed and moaned and the sweat gathered under the neckband of my mac and froze, and the cold got into a back tooth because of breathing through the mouth.

I'd worked out to myself that an hour might do it. I hastily revised the estimate to ninety minutes, which incidentally wasn't going to leave much time for decision the other end, and broke it down into six instalments of a quarter-hour each. I'd always needed to do that sort of thing, whether doing guard duty in the army or driving up the A.5 to see the folks. At the first quarter I said to myself, a sixth. Well, that was something. At the half-hour I said, a third, but with a heavier heart. I had just been through a bad patch and the prospect of twice as much again was numbing. At the three-quarters I cried triumphantly, halfway, and had a snorter from the flask. It tasted wonderful. On top of that, the lie of the ground suggested I was maybe rather better than half-way in reality.

So it proved. The first sign of man, an abandoned snow-covered coil of steel wire rope, came only twenty minutes later. More wire a bit later and suddenly a broken line of wooden stakes. Everything was covered with snow but the edges and angles of manmade things obtruded as distinctively as if they had been painted scarlet.

At ten thirty-four, which was exactly one hour and twenty-one minutes after leaving Joe, I had traversed the base of Fifeneset. To my right the ground once more sloped away down to the fjord. I was perhaps two hundred, perhaps three hundred, feet up. At the water's edge, a little further on, were the ruined remains of harbour buildings. Roughly level with me, on a kind of ledge on the snowy hillside, was a low building cut into the slope, and the skeleton of a cableway that had linked it to the installations below. I was looking at the one-time pride and joy of the Caledonian Spitsbergen Development Corporation, the Holyroodhamna iron mine.

But closer at hand — indeed only a couple of hundred yards away — was a hut which looked solid and four-square and which I decided was my prime objective. Things were turning out rather well. Nearly forty minutes remained until Joe's deadline, I might be back in comfort and safety sooner than I'd thought. I squelched towards the building. I was certain it was the wartime weather station. It had that army silhouette.

Besides, all meteorological stations were high up, weren't they? Roof of the Air Ministry, etc.

I half-circled it cautiously. In all reasonable probability Bland and Randers would have set out for Ny Alesund hours ago. After all, they were going to be up at five the next morning to call for me. But you never knew … it was just possible they might be sleeping here. I looked down to the fjord and could see no signs of a boat.

The far end of the hut was a ruin. The door was missing and half the roof reduced to bare, blackened spars. The windows gaped. The nearer end seemed to be in tolerable repair. The window apertures were roughly boarded up; the roof had been patched with, among other things, the missing door. The boarding-up meant that the hut was also fairly blind, which was useful. I crept up to the blindest window of all and listened carefully. Nothing. The door was old and askew and handleless, roughly fastened with a loop of wire; fastened from the outside — another good sign.

I hesitated. It was ten forty. I pulled the pistol out of my pocket, took a breath, and knocked on the door. Timidly the first time, then more loudly.

No reply.

I unhooked the loop of wire and pulled. The door creaked open and sagged to one side. Immediately, I had that indefinable feeling that the place was being inhabited. In the gloom I sought first, and located, the bunk. It was an ancient double-decker with only the lower deck made up. Otherwise there was a rough-hewn table, a rickety chair, lots of litter, old newspapers, and a musty smell.

I went on in. The mattress on the bunk was old and filthy but the blankets looked quite decent. The pillow was a soiled white shirt stuffed with rags or something. I looked up.

Hanging from a hook on the ceiling was a hurricane lamp, unrusty and comparatively clean. I tipped it. There was the faint splash of paraffin. In the corner by the door was an old oil-drum stove, still warm. I looked inside. A few embers glowed. What else?

Empty bottles, one smelling of ammonia. A battered kettle. An iron pot. Some empty food tins, all with Norwegian labels. Somebody was living here. Was it Bland, or Randers, or neither of them? The evidence hardly fitted either personality. Tarn had warned me that trappers made use of all and any accommodation on Svalbard. One of these might easily be squatting here. I looked at my watch: ten forty-three. Half an hour left. There was still time to take a quick peep at the mine.

I was just letting myself out when I noticed the tin ammunition box pushed under the bunk. I made a quick survey of the landscape outside and went back in. Looking into anyone's old hut was one thing; looking into someone's box was another. I slid it out and opened the lid. Camera, binoculars, books — the contents registered themselves in that order. The camera was a beauty, an Exakta. With it were all sorts of accessories; I didn't examine them closely, but certainly they included a small tripod with an elaborate head, extension tubes and what looked like a trip wire device, all carefully packed and looking somehow as if they hadn't been used very much. There was a film of dust on the lenses of the binoculars. I turned to the books.

I couldn't read a lot of the names. They were in faded tombstone lettering that was hard enough to interpret at the best of times. From the rest I picked out some sort of textbook on camp structures and another on *Freikorperkultur*; harmless enough. D'Annunzio in the original Italian. Nietzsche, Goethe, Thomas Carlyle (well! well!). Rosenberg's

Myth of the Twentieth Century… Short of *Mein Kampf* itself you couldn't have anything much more suspect than *that*. Wait a minute, here was something by Kossina, and one of the scraps of useless information I had picked up in my time concerned Kossina. He was an anthropologist with a nice line in race theories. Most of the Nazi race-myths had derived from Kossina. If some hermit were living here, he was no ordinary hermit; and certainly no ordinary trapper.

I straightened up. The time was ten fifty-two; I had expended nine precious minutes. Twenty-one left if I were to go back with Joe. I wondered anxiously if he would be able to see my signals from here. Perhaps it would be best to make them without more ado. The mine was another half-mile, anyway; there wouldn't be time to more than glance at it. I dithered for another three minutes, leaving eighteen. I started off, stopped irresolutely, and came back. A quarter of an hour now.

I broke open the pistol and reached in my pocket for the shells. The flask was in the way. I drew it out. That was all save for a few coins. I remembered then what had happened aboard the *Harriet*. I'd taken the cartridges out to make room for the flask and laid them down, meaning to put them in another pocket. In the fluster and embarrassment of being filmed I must have left them there. Ah well, that's show business.

CHAPTER THIRTY-THREE

There is something very off-putting about sneaking up to a hole in a mountain. You can't be sure what eyes might be watching you from just inside its blackness. I decided to approach it from above, or at least keeping well up on the slope, and not use the path from the weather station. The disadvantage was that the snow was exceptionally thick here, more than knee-deep. The legs of my trousers were freshly soaked. I remembered the virtual snowlessness of the valley at Longyear. It was odd what a difference an extra degree or two north could make.

At eleven thirteen, which was the official Time's Up, I paused with the intention of observing two minutes' silence in homage to what might have been and having a tiny refreshment. Even as the crunch of my feet in the snow ceased I heard something in the distance. Faintly borne on the wind was the sound of a petrol engine. Could it be Joe, starting up for home? It was too cruel. But no, the note was different, pitched lower, sounding steadier. And anyway the wind was blowing the wrong way. I went on a few paces. The noise was slightly louder. Twenty or thirty paces and it was louder still. It wasn't Joe and it didn't need much imagination to guess where it was coming from.

The slope here had a slight convexity which meant I had temporarily lost sight of the mine. Then all at once I was on top of it and the noise was the loudest noise in the world. A puff of blue smoke from the rusty iron roof below confirmed its source. The building was dilapidated but the walls and superstructure were still standing. A massive flywheel projected from the front. Evidently it had been the winding house, either for the railway inside the mine or the cable way down to the fjord, or both.

In a way the sudden approach made things easier. I had no opportunity to indulge in hesitation. I stopped instinctively then went quickly up to the near wall. Standing on tiptoe I could see through a gaping hole under the eaves. The inside was shadowed and chaotic. I could just pick out the mine opening on the left and a good deal of derelict machinery in the centre. The petrol engine seemed to be in the furthest recesses.

I dropped on to my heels and went cautiously round to the front. The ground here was much trampled; the footpath from the weather station continued on and down, in a zigzag route to the little harbour below. The remains of the cableway took a direct and precipitate plunge to the same destination. About half the façade of the winding house was open to the wind and weather. I edged along to the aperture and took another look in. From this aspect the mouth of the mine showed up more plainly, a black hole in the mountain side crudely squared off with timber baulks. I ventured inside. The noise of the engine was really close now, running very evenly. It sounded like a pump or generator. I went up to the tunnel mouth and looked down. What daylight there was in the winding house reached about forty feet into the shaft, revealing a mud floor, grey and smooth, and in the centre the receding rusty rails of the old railway. Then blackness save for a distant point of orange light. It was a generator.

Obviously someone was down there. Logically it was the hermit from the weather station, whoever that might prove to be. Well, he couldn't see me unless he were on his way out now and I were standing directly in the tunnel mouth — which

I was! I stepped aside hurriedly. The generator was in the far corner, partly hidden by debris; a little horizontal engine in a rusty metal frame; possibly of army origin. The exhaust tube poked up through a hole in the roof.

I sat down at a strategic point where I would hear anyone coming out of the shaft without being silhouetted myself against the entrance, and unsnapped the chafing collar of the plastic mac. My feet were like lumps of ice and my nasal passages smarted. At least it was out of the breeze here.

I lit a cigarette. It tasted extraordinarily strong and savoury and the smoke hung in clouds of pure colour, an intense powdery light blue. I was dully admiring the effect when it dawned on me that it was a certain give-away if anyone should emerge. I pinched out the cigarette and waved my arms to dispel the smoke. It hung there, obstinately, eddying in front of the shaft. In the half-light the colour might go unnoticed, in the virgin Arctic air the smell would surely betray me. Finally it began to thin and drift away.

What next? The mine mouth gaped a challenge. If I kept close to either wall, I could perhaps venture a little way in without danger, though I had never liked holes in the ground much; not even the Bakerloo Line. I sidled up to the timber baulks. A dead, dry coldness seemed to float from the shaft. The distant pinpoint of light glowed feebly. Was it five amps fifty yards away, or fifty amps at five hundred yards? Pressing myself against the left-hand side of the shaft I took ten deliberate steps and paused. Silence. Or was that a *tingle* in the air? Something elusive, scarcely perceptible. Ten more steps. I wished my shoes wouldn't jar so on the hard mud. I strained my ears. It was more like the *memory* of a sound than a sound itself; like a phrase that someone has said to you when you're preoccupied and miles away and don't hear; then seconds later, when you're surfacing, you catch the words still ringing in your head and say 'What?'

I went forward again. Now it was clearer: an aural illusion, of course. The distorted amplification of some mechanical sound. Drilling, perhaps. I looked back. The outside world was bright and inviting.

Another yard, tentatively now. Then it came again, a faint crescendo. Illusion hell! It was real enough, and I didn't like it one bit. In fact I'd had more than enough. Without turning I backed and side-stepped out the way I'd come.

What I had heard was music, and what's more it was music I knew: the trombone lament from Berlioz's *Symphonic Funèbre et Triomphale*.

CHAPTER THIRTY-FOUR

I got out of the winding house altogether and scuffed up the snow slope behind to a pile of fallen stones which would give me cover. I was appalled. Berlioz has no greater admirer, but midnight in an abandoned iron mine miles from anywhere was not the time and place for appreciating him to the full. I decided to wait and observe whoever came out of the mine, if he chose to do so within half an hour. After that I would make fresh plans. Meanwhile I was cold and sodden and miserable. I had a consoling nip from the flask and lit the half-cigarette I had pinched out.

From my vantage point I surveyed the scenery. Too late I realized my pioneering progress from ancient weather hut to ancient mine had left a straggly line of footprints in the snow. Ah well, if the hermit noticed, he noticed. It was the least of my worries.

I made myself as comfortable as possible and waited.

At twenty past midnight the sky was at its flattest, greyest and dimmest, and the sound of the generator stopped with a couple of coughs. I ducked behind my stones and watched. There were faint sounds of movement from inside the winding house, and after a minute a figure emerged and trudged off past me towards the weather station.

It was not Bland, nor was it Randers.

It was almost certainly an old man, once tall but now bent. He walked with a sad, imprecise gait, his head down. He was wearing an old peaked hat with the flaps down, a long overcoat, and great rubber boots of glaring red. So this was the hermit! I watched him until the bulge in the slope hid him from view, then slithered down to the winding house. From there I watched him re-emerge and continue along the trodden path, a stiff, dwindling little figure seeming so frail that a gust of wind would send it spinning into the fjord far below.

The thing now was to inspect the mine shaft in peace. That was it. I said it to myself several times in an off-hand, matter-of-fact kind of voice. I could have the generator going. If I hadn't heard the motor when I was at the weather hut, his old ears surely wouldn't. But I waited until I saw him enter the distant hut and gave him half an hour on top of that to get off to sleep, using part of the time to peel off my wringing wet socks, rub my feet with a few drops of Scotch (it was worth it) and put on the dry pair I'd brought. Morale took an upward curl. I hung the wet socks up to dry.

It was one thirty-two a.m. Sunday. The *Bellsund* would be approaching Ny Alesund by now; might even be berthed already. If my absence weren't detected until five a.m. I had a safe five hours before Bland and Co. could arrive. If they found out straight away I still had two hours anyway.

The generator had been further concealed by rubbish. That must have been what the old man had been doing in the winding house before leaving. I uncovered it again, fitted the starting crank and turned on the petrol tap. No point in further delay. It was one thirty-five. I swung the crank. The engine started. My God! They'd hear that in Murmansk, never mind a mile away. After a moment it settled. I nipped over to the aperture and kept an agonized watch on the weather station. No immediate sign of activity. I waited a long ten minutes. Still nothing.

The moment had come. I went briskly into the tunnel for a good thirty yards and listened. Then another twenty. One bar of Berlioz and I was off. But there was no sound in the cold, musty stillness of the air. I went on. The incline became steeper, but never uncomfortably so. The distant light rapidly grew nearer and presently a second one beckoned. They were only tiny bulbs, not more than ten or fifteen watts; just enough to cast small pools of light in the immediate vicinity and show the way. Looking back from the third one I could no longer see the reassuring light of day from the tunnel mouth.

The walls of the mine were mostly invisible. From the isolated patch of illumination they appeared to be regular and well cut. Though I instinctively kept my head low, the roof was adequately high for as far as I penetrated, shored with timber props. The floor was smooth, which was just as well. Once my foot caught something metallic which went tinkling off to one side. I spent two minutes fumbling around the floor in the dark before I found it and put it in my last vacant pocket, the little waistband one. It felt as if it might be a badge. The air was like refrigerated breath. It brought back a holiday impression from somewhere I couldn't quite place.

After the third light I sensed that the decline was levelling off. In all there were twelve lights before I stopped and I counted forty-two paces between one pair and fifty between another. The earlier ones might have been a bit closer because of the curve of the incline. I went perhaps four hundred yards into the mountain side in all.

Three things brought me to a halt. The first was that beyond the twelfth light the floor of the mine became broken and strewn with rubble. The second was that further on in the gloom the shaft appeared to fork into two divergent tunnels, low and primitive, as if the miners had lost their vein of haematite and were prospecting for it again. The third thing was that parked under the twelfth light, at the terminus of the rail tracks, was one of the old trolleys that had been used in the mine — bogies, they call them in Scotland. And on the bogie rested the white coffin.

There could be no mistake. The clumsy, dribbled letters were still on the side. Handle with Reverence, Peter had translated. Reverently or otherwise someone had done some pretty strenuous handling since the coffin disappeared beneath a mound of stones in Ny Alesund little more than thirty-six hours before.

Gingerly I tried the lid. At least I had to make the effort. To my relief it was secure. Who had moved the late Mr Williams seemed obvious. I had a good idea why they'd done it. How they'd managed the feat remains one of the unsolved mysteries of the whole business, along with the exact identity of the Mystery Caller and the fate of ... but I am anticipating. It must have been done at dead of night, even if dead of night in the Arctic summer means broad daylight.

I stooped down and tried to peer up the two low tunnels. The one to the left showed only blackness. The one to the right seemed to terminate in a faint glow, but pinkish rather than the yellow illumination of the other lights. I stood up and felt for the electric cable. It led up on the right-hand shaft. I sniffed. The holiday impression sorted itself out. Trier on a cold March morning's sightseeing, and the crypt beneath the St Matthew Basilica. Wasn't that it? Perhaps I should nerve myself for a final effort and crawl along the low shaft to the faint pink radiance. Curiosity and plain funk fought inside me. I was still pondering, when all the lights flickered once and went out. I prayed, 'Oh God, no, please no.'

CHAPTER THIRTY-FIVE

The first objective was to get my back against something. That had been the rule when I had to creep and scuttle upstairs to bed in the prosaic but night-haunted little house in Lichfield twenty-five years before. It still held good. I stretched an arm behind me and inched back until I felt the cold mine wall. The darkness was total. To my left the shaft sloped up and away to the outside world. The white coffin was two feet away to my right. I could see nothing. I listened and could hear only the thumping of my pulse.

What had happened? The old man had come back. Or *they* had come back. They would be stealthily advancing along the shaft. Any minute now the light from torches would shine out in the dark. Suddenly I was lurching away from the spot where I had stopped, frenziedly determined not to be caught in a dead end. Niches, niches, that was what I needed. There were always niches in the walls of mines for the miners to stand in while the trolleys went by. I stretched both arms wide and stumbled along lunging at each side.

They were uniformly smooth. No niche for Colin. I stopped, panting, and tried to pull myself together. That's what they had said at school — 'Pull Yourself Together, Boy,' as if you'd started to unwrap or something. One thing I knew: I wasn't going to retreat up either of the two rat-holes into which the mine divided. That was for sure. I forced myself to reason. If it was the old hermit on his own, I ought to be able to deal with him. If it was Bland — I couldn't think of the clownish Randers as an adversary — the situation could be uncomfortable. But it was still early for Bland.

I held my watch up close to my eyes. The phosphorescence was old and chipped. I could just read the time. It was two. A nasty thought occurred: there would hardly have been time for the old man to get all the way back from the weather hut. Assume it was Bland. There was a chance he might still be unsuspicious. Perhaps he had slept somewhere at hand and was only now about to set out to collect me at Ny Alesund. Perhaps he thought the lights had been left on by accident and had merely switched them off in passing… Or supposing the lights went on again now, this minute. I might be standing right under one, floodlit. I wished I had a torch. My God! What about my wet socks hung up in the winding house for all to see?

The safest point would be midway between two lights. Pressed to the tunnel wall I might even escape detection there altogether. But how to locate a mid-way point was the problem. I trod warily back the way I had fled, one hand on the wall, one hand outstretched ahead, until I touched the white coffin again. This was definitely under a light. Half of fifty was twenty-five. I took twenty-five paces up the shaft again and pressed against the wall, trying to be thin, breathing deeply of the nasty air to calm my pulse. The sweat was trickling coldly down my sides. I still had on the plastic mac, like a sausage skin. I listened. Was that the distant murmur of voices? Gone again. I decided to remain stock still for quarter of an hour. No, for twelve minutes, which would bring the time to two twenty. That was reasonable. If anyone were coming down the mine they would be here by then.

It was a long vigil, made longer still by my usual clockwatching tactics. I tried counting, guessing, estimating, dividing. After a while I hit on the idea of treating each minute as an hour and the whole period as a twelve-hour day. It was now quarter past three … half past … quarter to four … four … put the kettle on for tea … only got to stay up till midnight. Finally I told myself it was Time, and in fact it was two twenty-two a.m., which was two minutes past Time. I set off up the shaft fairly sanguinely. In the comfort of Nothing Happening I began to feel more confident.

When the outside world showed as a pale but welcoming radiance I proceeded more cautiously. It would be silly to blunder unnecessarily into trouble. I took the last fifty yards very circumspectly indeed, freezing at every step and breathing through wide-open mouth, which was quieter than through the nose.

At the threshold I waited a full two minutes. No sound. I marched steadfastly into the full refulgence of the winding house.

There was no one there.

My socks were where I had left them hanging. I snatched them up. Nothing else seemed to have changed. I bent over the generator and jiggled the little primer above the carburettor. There was no sign or smell of petrol. I unscrewed the cap on the tank and squinted inside. It was empty.

The path down to the fjord was an elongated hairpin reducing the gradient of the hillside to a manageable one in eight or thereabouts. I walked openly down it. The first part of the first leg was in full view of the weather hut, and I had those mild shivers in the back you experience if you cross a road too slowly and know a bus is going to sweep by just behind you. But I wasn't really worrying. All danger seemed to have evaporated in the ridiculous anticlimax of the Plunge into Inky Blackness. I was almost light-headed with relief. What a bloody fool trick!

It was three ten as I reached the water's edge and the old Arctic day-night, of which I was beginning to tire, was perceptibly more matitudinal. There was even a suspicion of sun somewhere. I had been hoping for enough shelter to have a nap; the prospect wasn't very promising. Two of the three old buildings were roofless wrecks. The third was better but was surrounded by rubbish and smelled evilly. Down at sea-level the snow was once again absent.

The remains of a timber-piled jetty jutted into the water; drawn up in its lee was a shabby little boat, something like a punt. I wondered whether to steal it and make off, and rejected the idea immediately. I wouldn't get anywhere and anyway there was no point now. My feet were cold and damp again and swallowing had become rather alarming. My eyes smarted with fatigue. I sat on an abandoned cable drum, had the last of the whisky, and dissolved an aspirin on the tongue. The sense of release began to fade. I hadn't accomplished much. In fact I had been pretty ineffectual.

The bit of body-snatching was the most conclusive evidence I'd found. It would also sound a very tall story if and when I tried to pass it on to anyone. 'Well, I tell you, there in this mine was the chap who was supposed to have been buried in Ny Alesund two days before…' I would need to take someone to see it. There were the books by Rosenberg and Kossina, the *Herrenvolk*ethnologist. Again no portable evidence. That reminded me. I reached into the waistband pocket and drew out the thing I had kicked in the mine.

It wasn't bad. It wasn't bad at all. It was a death's-head badge with the motto emblazoned below, *Mein Ehre Heisst Treue*. Well, well, well, the old S.S. It was unsubtle evidence, and possibly explainable-away, but it would do for the time being.

The sun actually peeped out of a break in the clouds and the waters of the fjord sparkled. I had an idea and went down to the little old boat. It was quite dry inside. I lay down and made myself as cosy as I could and covered my eyes with my handkerchief and presently drifted in and out of sleep.

I woke with a start. The sun was stronger. I sat up. I had a terrible dry mouth and a worse headache. An experimental swallow was only moderately reassuring. The time was six thirty. It was Sunday. I looked about me. No movement up the hill. But down the fjord, close inshore and just recognizable against the blur of the horizon, was the bow wave of an approaching boat.

There was still plenty of time to move, and all the compulsion in the world to do so. But I sat on in the punt. I hadn't decided yet how to play the next scene. Assuming it was Bland, and I hardly dared hope otherwise, I had to behave very innocently. Any suspicion of secret-service stuff would be suicidal. Equally, there was no point in remaining an absolute sitter of a target if he was coming armed and purposeful. I took advantage of a cloud obscuring the sun for five minutes to leave the boat and retreat into the biggest of the buildings. Only one gaunt truss remained of the roof, and the inside was just a bit of landscape, but I could see from it without being seen.

CHAPTER THIRTY-SIX

The vessel came nearer. It was smaller than I had first thought, only an open motorboat. That was disappointing. The official launches of the Governor and the Chief Inspector of Mines were in the sea-going class. Hopes, never very buoyant, that it might be an ally quietly sank. I stared out from my hiding place trying to identify who was aboard. If Randers were with Bland, I could be fairly sanguine. If not — I had a spasm of panic. Our meeting would be ugly, probably more. I had no escape, no defence. I tried desperately to un-wish the whole thing, imagine that it had never happened. Then I thought I saw the bobble of Randers's woolly cap, and morale lifted. The important thing was to behave naturally, however I did behave. To be caught skulking would be disastrous.

The last fifty yards of the boat's progress were out of my sight. I heard the motor note subside and then the bump and scrape of the hull alongside the jetty. After a moment — and I couldn't help holding my breath — a head bobbed into view, then the whole man. It was Bland. He was wearing rugged outdoor clothes and his expression wasn't encouraging. But behind him tagged Randers, looking worried. It would be all right.

Bland stopped and looked around. Then he called out.

'Mr Panton, Mr Panton. You are here?'

I counted fifteen and advanced slowly into the light, rubbing my eyes and yawning. They stood motionless, silent.

'Oh, there you are,' I said lamely. 'I'm afraid I went to sleep waiting for you. I was up all night.'

'I am not sure I understand.' Bland's voice was icy.

'At a party,' I said. 'Aboard the *Harriet*. It was quite a night.' Randers's mouth twitched nervously into the old grin, then dropped again.

Bland said, 'And how are you here now?'

'They dropped me here before going north again. Didn't you get my message?' I managed to sound aggrieved.

'We heard merely that you had been taken off the *Bellsund* by the hunting party. The wireless officer has told us.'

I bet he did. 'But he also told you that I would meet you here? Surely he told you that?'

Bland hesitated. 'Not exactly — he was not sure where you would be.'

'Tt-tt.' I clicked annoyance. 'I informed the captain exactly what the plan was. I can't think why it wasn't passed on to you.'

A simple ploy but it seemed to work. Bland was thrown off his attack. Randers cheered up.

'I thought Col would not have acted so mysteriously,' he beamed. 'Have you waited long?'

'About an hour and a half,' I said. I'd worked that one out in advance. I had to allow enough time for the *Harriet* to have got clear. Besides, there were activities of my own that had to be accommodated. Bland was already studying my bedraggled trouser-legs and ski boots scoured clean of colour by the snow.

I glanced down at them ruefully. 'I went for a walk. To clear my head. It was silly, I suppose.'

Bland kept his face impassive, but his eyes were colder than ever.

'Along the water for a little way,' I expounded, 'and then right up the hill there.' I flung out my arm roughly in the direction of the mine. 'It was most interesting…'

I broke off. High up on the slope, moving along the path from the weather station, was the black dot of a human being. The Hermit!

If Bland noticed him he didn't reveal it. He said, 'I am glad you enjoyed it. Unfortunately it has rather upset our plans for today, not knowing whether we would find you here or not. I am afraid we must soon return to Ny Alesund. If you wish to see the site for our camp we must waste no more time.'

He led the way up from the water's edge, stamping his feet on the ground. He was wearing plus-four trousers tucked into thick woollen stockings. His boots were massive and studded. His calves were very solid.

Just beyond the ruined buildings was a level patch of ground a hundred or two hundred yards long and fifty wide, free of snow. 'This is where the main encampment will be,' said Bland. 'The buildings we will try and restore as stores and perhaps a dining hall. There will be no dormitories — not at first, anyway. Our young people will live in tents. If the youths from Cambridge can do it, ours can also.'

Randers nodded sagely in agreement. 'Nice place, Col?'

'Very nice.'

'There is a spring of fresh water,' Bland continued, 'but we would also build a cistern upon the mountain side. We are told that although the snow lies all the year up there the water will still collect.'

I took a peek up the hill. The black dot was a black ant now, and about to reach the mine-workings.

'Down there by the water,' said Bland, pointing, 'we will repair and enlarge the jetty, so that quite large ships can come direct with our campers — or better still, seaplanes. Up on the headland' — now he was indicating the bulge of Fifeneset —

'we will have a lookout post to see that no one gets into trouble out in the fjord.'

I looked up the hillside again, deliberately this time. The Hermit had vanished, presumably into the mine. 'And the mine?'

'Perhaps for storage purposes. It is not very safe. The roof is already fallen in some way inside. The machinery house we might be able to use.'

In this fashion we slowly ascended, Bland cataloguing the various natural assets of the place, until we reached the elbow bend in the path down from the mine. The Hermit had come out of the winding house and was hurrying on down towards us. It seemed to me that he was anxious, but maybe it was imagination. Socks, I'd recovered the socks. Had there been anything else?

'In that direction, beyond the lonely hut you see over there,' Bland was saying, 'there is a fine ski slope for beginners. Don't forget, Mr Panton, we shall hope in time to have young men and girls from lands where they never have seen a mountain.' He must have seen the Hermit by now; Randers too, but neither made any immediate comment.

'Up here,' Bland went on, 'away from the smoke and decay of Europe we will make a *fountain*, Mr Panton. A fountain for the refreshment of youth. New strength, new life, new purity will flow from here.' His eyes were taking on the visionary gleam I had noticed off Grumantbyen that night. 'These slopes, Mr Panton, will echo to the sound of young strong voices in all the tongues of Europe. You approve, Mr Panton?'

'To be honest,' I said, 'that kind of thing has never appealed to me one bit.'

The Hermit was now seventy yards off.

Bland shrugged. 'I am not surprised. You are an indoor bird, eh, Mr Panton? You are the old Europe. You are like the Roman Empire in decline: civilized and tolerant and — how do you put it? — easy-going. You are a nice fellow. You will doubtless die in your bed. I hope so. But your children … they will perhaps not. You have children?'

'No.' The discussion seemed very academic.

'There is still time. Your children will perhaps not die in their beds. Because the barbarians will be at the gates of Rome by then, Mr Panton, and their faces will be black — or yellow.'

Fifty yards. I looked at Randers. His face was wearing a sort of fixed attentiveness to Bland I had seen before, but no special tension.

'Unless,' said Bland, 'a new, strong Europe can rise to defend itself. Perhaps it will rise from here.'

'If they start dropping hydrogen bombs there isn't going to be anything left to defend.'

Forty yards.

'I do not believe that will happen, myself. If it should, then Spartapol will be more important than ever. Up here a cadre of New Europeans can escape whatever befalls. In the mine there, and perhaps others like it, they will be safe even from — what is it? Yes, fallout. We can strengthen them and make ventilation plant. There is much work. Our young people will have to work hard as well as play hard when they come here. But hard work will not harm them. Excuse me.'

He stepped three, four, five paces forward to meet the Hermit. They spoke rapidly, in low tones. The Hermit seemed excited about something and twice pointed back the way he had come. I held my breath.

Randers said idly, 'You didn't meet the Professor Fieseler?'

'What?' His words hadn't registered.

'This man here. The bird-watcher. He is a scientist who comes here every year to study the birds.'

Bland was turning. His face was as calm as ever. 'Mr Panton,' he said, 'may I introduce you?'

CHAPTER THIRTY-SEVEN

Whatever had been bothering the old man, it wasn't anything he connected with me. His handshake was perfunctory, his hand feeling cold and calloused, and his gaze averted.

'Professor Fieseler comes each year to make his observations,' said Bland. 'Naturally we have often met. Fortunately his work here will be completed before our young desperadoes disturb the wild life too much!'

The Hermit looked up momentarily, as if something Bland said had touched him on a sore spot. I looked into sunken, tired eyes over big folds of skin and I had a fleeting sensation that I'd encountered him somewhere before. We had turned and were descending the path again. The old man came too. He was still anxious to communicate something to Bland. They lagged behind, the Hermit's voice jabbering away in low, querulous tones.

Randers said, 'Will it be a nice camp, Col?'

'Could be. But not for everyone. It sounds as if young chaps with black or yellow faces won't be exactly welcomed. How about Jews?'

'I don't knao about that. I will find out.'

'Did you take some lovely pictures yesterday?'

'The day before, it was. Yes, very nice. The little Finnish miss has come over to represent the spirit of youth.'

'Were they — saucy?'

'Oh, nao, Col. Ha, ha, you are making fun. But we have taken our "pin-ups", yes.'

We regained the level patch where the camp would be. I turned to watch the other two come up. Bland was now ahead, the old Hermit trailing about a pace after him, tall and bent. Again I had the transient impression that I'd seen him before. For a fraction of a second I felt I was on the verge of placing him, then the identification wriggled away. Think, think!

'Mr Randers.' Bland drew him aside to murmur something. Randers nodded vigorously. It was like the plotters confabbing in *Un Ballo in Maschera*.

I said to the Hermit in German, 'I understand you are an ornithologist. I am so pleased to have met you.'

He replied in so low and gruff a voice that I could only catch a *Dankeschoen*. Still, that was something.

'I, too, am an ornithologist,' I continued. 'Only an amateur, of course.' I laughed modestly. 'This morning early I have been for a walk here and seen so many interesting birds.'

'Ja?' A spark of interest.

I sieved hastily through what I could recall from the bird book. 'Yes indeed. For example, I have seen a pair of Little Stints — *Calidris minuta* — and their young. I was so excited.'

'Ja.' The interest had gone. Perhaps I'd got the wrong word. I'd translated Little Stint as Kleine Stint. He should have got the Latin, though.

I pressed on. 'But the most interesting bird of all I could not identify. You see, it was dead. I felt so sad for it. Perhaps the long journey from the south had been too much.'

It was a silly boys' story allegory. I wasn't sure what I was aiming at. The old head lifted slightly as if the word 'dead' had touched him and he grunted something I didn't catch. The monstrous red boots thudded on the path. I lit a cigarette. At the end of the level plain we came to a halt again. Bland turned and to my surprise clapped me on the back. It was the last thing I had been expecting.

'Well, Mr Panton, can you any longer disapprove of our plan? Visualize the scene! The laughter and the shouting. The young bodies in the sunlight and fresh air. Breathe, Mr Panton, it is the freshest air in the world!'

Obediently I breathed. The cigarette smoke was sucked down somewhere it shouldn't have been sucked and I collapsed in an agony of coughing. When I looked up through streaming eyes Bland's unlined face held so much scorn and derision that I wanted to kick him in the crutch.

'On the contrary,' I croaked. 'I think it's the lousiest idea since the Children's Crusade.'

Bland smiled without malice. 'Fortunately for our friendship your approval — which was never essential — is now no longer even relevant. I have heard by radio that final sanction is being granted in Oslo and London tomorrow.'

So that was why he was so jovial. 'I see.'

'That is not all, Mr Panton.' He couldn't resist his moment of triumph. 'Last night, just before I heard the news, a compatriot of yours has arrived. His attitude to our scheme was so much more favourable than your own that I could not resist regarding him as an omen of success! I tell you this so that you will not be offended if I should seem to prefer his help.' And again he clapped me on the back.

'Who? Who is it?'

'It is a little surprise for you, Mr Panton. You will see.'

'Who is it, Randers?'

'I am not sure, Col, I did not see.'

We boarded the motorboat. Its hull was a faded blue. There were two cockpits. I got in the rear one with Randers. Bland started the engine and we backed out into the fjord. On the hillside the old Hermit was toiling back towards the mine.

CHAPTER THIRTY-EIGHT

The ride back was pleasant, and would have been pleasanter still in other circumstances. Bland kept close inshore and the cliffs were alive with seabirds. At the square headland which divided Krossfjorden and Kingsbay the sea was choppy. Bland took a wide sweep and settled on to a long diagonal run across to Ny Alesund. The wind was fresh but the sun warm. The boat skipped on the waves and the blue smoke from the engine hung briefly over the wake before the wind took it.

I wedged myself on the hard seat and let my eyes close. I dozed on and off, waking with dry mouth and lolling head. Sometimes I watched Randers's profile as he gazed fixedly ahead. From this angle his nose was absurdly upturned. His hair was parted by the wind, revealing the long recession right to the crown.

'Christ, you slight man,' I thought. 'You banana.' At the same time I despised myself for despising him. What was Randers; who was he? I'd never tried to get to know him properly. Well, he was well cast as anyone's front man. He was the type, all right. The patient, pleasant, unsuccessful sort, hired to be nice to everyone over the canapés at the Dorchester. We'd had one for *Simon*. Your friend if you were in the mood to be nice back, someone to kick if you weren't. Yet there are not many human faces you can look at without detecting a certain trace of beat-up nobility. I saw it now on Randers's face, in the weary set of his mouth and the terrible incongruity of his nose. Perhaps if I had trusted him and confided in him we could have been allies. I kicked him on the shin.

'Who is this man who's arrived?'

'I have said, Col, I don't knao. He came on the Governor's launch late last night.'

The skyline of Ny Alesund was dominated by the shabby bulk of the *Bellsund*. I remembered how small she had looked at Tromsø. Now she looked like an Atlantic liner. And nearly as big, ten times more rakish, partly hidden behind her, was the Governor's launch. Bland hadn't fibbed. I closed my eyes. I didn't want to arrive. Arrival meant more muddle, more thinking, more explaining, more manoeuvring, more alleging. I would have liked to stay for ever in the dancing boat in the sun. I dozed again.

Bland went in upstream of the landing stage, at a smaller jetty. There were four or five other craft there, mostly open boats, old and stout and painted in these faded hues. As we clambered ashore Bland took my arm. His hand was like a clamp.

'We shall meet again in the saloon of the *Bellsund*,' he said. 'Perhaps in about one hour's time. I think we shall have a little ceremony that will be most interesting.'

I wagged my head and trudged off to the ship. At the landing stage I turned to see if the stone cairn over the late Mr Williams was still there. It was, of course. Randers was following dejectedly behind. I let him catch up.

'Was the man a big man with a red face and hair at the back of his head like Sir Winston Churchill?'

'No, no. It is a younger man. I do not know the name.'

We went in silence to our cabin. I resisted a craving to throw myself on my bunk and plugged in my shaver instead. Randers began to pack his things into a lurid off-white case. He put them in slowly and meticulously. I watched each item. They were bits of him that had been around all voyage but I was noticing them now for the first time: the cream shirts with long pointed collars, the sand-coloured shoes, the bottles and brushes and fat leather writing case. It reminded me of the cabin-maid putting away Dancer's things. I switched off the shaver.

'Where are you going?'

'I am staying here, Col, for ten days. Until the next voyage of the *Bellsund*. Then the Dr Bland and I will rejoin her to go and see the northern sights we have missed this time. Have you enjoyed them?'

I didn't answer. 'Why are you staying?'

'Because we have much work to do with the sheem. Dr Bland has obtained permission from the deputy inspector of mines for me to stay.'

'Look,' I said. 'How much do you know about this bloody sheem?'

'What do you mean? I knao what I have told you. And it is not bloody.'

'Isn't it? All right.' I switched on the shaver again.

When I finished, Randers said diffidently, 'I have developed some pictures yesterday. Would you like to see?'

'If you like.'

He was holding a little sheaf of contact prints in strips of four. 'No one had an enlarger in Ny Alesund,' he explained.

The first ones were taken on the *Bellsund*. Peter and Maia gazing into the limitless distance. Peter and Maia laughing in the wind. Peter and Maia planning a brave new world. Peter and Maia on the hatch-cover. Peter and Maia with hands clasped and eyes shining. Ilse came into a couple of early ones and you could just see my foot in the corner of another.

'My foot,' I said. 'You'll have to amputate that, mate.'

The second batch was the one taken at the Spartapol site. I was conscious of a fluttering feeling as I took the first strip. It was all right. Maia was in trousers, boots, anorak. She was standing on a high headland — presumably Fifeneset — or scrambling up steep slopes. Next was a sequence with skis. Then she was in shorts and shirt. I hadn't seen the shorts before. Randers had evidently been using a filter and the contrast between snow and sky and clothes and complexion was dramatic. She looked marvellous. She was running by the water's edge, short fair hair tossing and shining. She was examining some tortuously-shaped log of driftwood. She was in the little skiff I had slept in, manipulating a single scull.

'Finally,' said Randers, 'here are our "pin-ups".'

I breathed out. Maia was in a one-piece black bathing costume, the practical unalluring kind they use in competitive swimming. Even so it clung to her little figure in a disturbing way. She was splashing in the shallows at the edge of the fjord and posing more stiffly in conventional attitudes of sun and air-worship. Randers was a good technician: there were pictures so plastic and yet so crisp that I could sense — rather than see — the soft fair hairs on smooth limbs.

The last strip of all was a change of mood. I frowned. Maia now stood in idealized attitudes like a patriotic artist's model. Across her breast was a sash with 'SPARTAPOL' in Gothic letters. In her hand was a staff with a silken banner which in one picture fluttered in the breeze enough to show the emblem of a mountain and a star enclosed in a Greek-key border.

'This one we will certainly use, I think,' said Randers.

As I gave him the pictures back I noticed the blisters on his outstretched hands. 'How did you get those?'

He turned his palm inwards so the worst of them wouldn't show. 'Oh, they are not bad. We were taking some equipment across the Spartapol site yesterday.'

'Of course. You told me you were going to. But I still don't understand how you did it?'

'Did what?' His face was wary.

I took the plunge. 'Dug up the coffin and replaced the stones and got it across the fjord without anyone seeing you.'

'I don't knao what you are talking about.' But he had gone white — literally, dramatically, suddenly, in a way that I'd never believed happened except to people who'd been mixing gin and cider and were about to heave up.

'And who or what's inside the thing? What are you up to, for God's sake?'

'Col, this is such nonsense.'

'Nonsense! Nonsense is it? By Christ, we'll see if it's nonsense! I bet you know what's going on. I bet you know it all.' I could feel another of those awful little fits of stuttering fury coming on.

'Col, please, I…'

'Oh, shut up, You make me sick.' I added more sanely, 'I only sense it. You must *know* by now. For Christ's sake, man, didn't you have enough of this last time? How old are you? Thirty-five? Forty? You must have qualified for the full curriculum. Now you're going to let another generation of poor little bastards in for the same. Honestly, I don't understand you.'

I picked up a towel and swept off to the shower. When I returned he had gone.

CHAPTER THIRTY-NINE

In the saloon, Gregg, the deputy leader of the Cambridge expedition, was reclining on the long seat that ran under the windows. He was propped up with pillows and his left leg was stretched out in a plastic splint.

'Hallo there,' he said. 'Behold the prize mug of the Cambridge and Exeter Svalbard '55 Expedition.'

'What happened?'

'Slipped and cracked my blasted tibia — and do you know when?'

'No.'

'Actually disembarking. Actually setting foot in the bloody place. I was trying to get a theodolite ashore at the same time. They took me straight back to the Governor's launch, so I was there for about five minutes. It must be a record.'

'Hard luck,' I said, sorting out the ways this might help me.

'Luckily we had a quack in the party. He fixed it, but they might keep me in the hospital at Longyear for a fortnight. I'm going on with you in the *Bellsund* this evening. The Governor's boat has to stand by for something else.'

'Well, I'm awfully sorry you hurt yourself but in a way I'm also glad. I need some moral support urgently.'

'Glad to oblige. After all, you were in the Corps, weren't you? *Honi Soit Qui Mal y Pense* and all that.'

The steward was bringing me some breakfast. I gulped down a cup of marvellous tea the colour of tomato soup.

'Right,' I said. 'I won't start at the beginning or anything, and bother you with minor mysteries like why anyone should want to take long-playing records to the Arctic, least of all of Berlioz's *Symphonic Funèbre et Triomphale* —'

'Eh?'

'I'll just stick to what I saw this morning.' I waved at the window. 'Over there in Krossfjorden, where they want to make this camp.'

'Oh, yes. Dr Bland said he was going to take you over today.'

'You've seen him? When?'

'Last night. He came aboard the Governor's launch as soon as we came in. He was very nice. Had a look at my leg and said it would be fine. He's not a medical doctor, of course, but he said he'd seen a few fractures in his time. We had quite a long chat. Did you know he was quite a famous physicist? Expert on the Ionosphere and all that.'

'No, but…'

'Knew this part of the world from years ago; used to spend a lot of time at the observatory in Tromsø.'

'Well, you see…'

'And he worked on the V-2 rockets at the end of the war, you know. In his own subject, of course. Went to America afterwards and everything. Then gave it all up and went into teaching.'

'Really!' The conversation wasn't going the way I'd planned at all. Any other time I'd have been interested to hear all I could about Bland; just now there were more pressing matters. 'Well, I heard that he was a naval captain in charge of the weather service in Narvik…'

'Yes, that was earlier in the war. He told me about that, too.'

'Did he? Okay. Well, one of his weather stations is still there in Krossfjorden, right by the camp site. Quite a coincidence. And there's an old man living in it like a sort of hermit.'

Gregg wrinkled his brow. 'But surely that's the bird-watcher — what's his name? Something like Fiedler. Working on some genetics thing. Goes back every year to the same place to catch the same families.'

I gaped at him. 'On the level?'

'Sure. He was there last time I came on an expedition, which was two years ago. He travelled back to Tromsø with us on the *Bellsund* on the last trip of the season. He's well known.'

I rallied. 'Well if his genetics aren't any better than his ornithology I wouldn't give much for the research he's doing. I told him I'd seen a pair of Little Stints and young, and he never blinked. Now the Little Stint breeds just about everywhere *except* Spitsbergen.'

'You're a bird man yourself?'

'Not exactly. I've read the Penguin.'

'I see.' Ironically.

'All right, his books then. He's got a lot of stuff there that is indicative, anyway. Strong-arm romantics like d'Annunzio and racialists like Rosenberg and Kossina.'

'Eh?' He looked baffled.

I closed my eyes momentarily. 'Finally there's the old mine. I went in. They've got a little generator fixed up to light it and they're making a sort of … museum at the end. I heard the music.'

'You *what*?'

'I heard the music.'

'Wagner, I suppose.' It was a sharper piece of irony than I'd have expected from Gregg.

'No, Berlioz actually. You see, it's to be a European thing, not just German. And there's this man Williams who was supposed to have been buried here a couple of days ago. They must have dug him up again. They've got him over there in the mine.'

Gregg looked at me steadily. He didn't laugh. I'll give him that.

'You honestly expect me to believe all this?'

'Yes.'

'I'm sorry, old chap. I can't. You've got too tired and been losing too much sleep. It's easy in this infernal daylight round the clock. You've started imagining things.'

'I wish I had.'

'Look, this Spartapol scheme, or whatever it's called, is not everyone's cup of tea, I grant you. I mean, I was never one for Scout camps and so on myself. Much happier going off on the bike with just a couple of good chums. But there are a lot of people who are very much in favour.'

'Yeah, I know. Someone Very High. Rather in his line.'

'So Bland was hinting last night.'

The hour since we had landed back at Ny Alesund was already up. I said, 'Will you come with me and take a look? — Oh, of course, you can't.' I'd forgotten about his leg. I shrugged. 'It's probably too late, anyway. They'll have collapsed a chunk of roof by now to seal it all off. And for ten or twenty years this bloody Spartapol will be no more than it seems. Then one day, when the time is right, they'll open up that little museum or whatever it is and start a thing going.'

Suddenly I saw another way out. It might work. It could work. It *had* to work. I said, 'But if you back me up we might still be able to frighten the Norwegians. There's a deputy inspector of mines around. I suspect Bland's going to produce him any minute for some ceremony he's planning. We could go bald-headed for him and at least get him to have a look under that cairn of stones. What do you say?'

Gregg shook his head. 'Forget it, old chap. Why don't you get some sleep? You look all in.'

CHAPTER FORTY

They came trooping into the saloon a minute later; all together as if they'd assembled elsewhere first. Bland held the door open for the deputy inspector of mines. Maia followed, in the red skirt and fluffy sweater. Ilse. Bland himself, letting the door swing to. Finally Randers, having to push it open again. He was carrying his camera and gear.

'Ah, you have found one another,' cried Bland, cockily. He might have planned it all, letting Gregg and me meet first so that the rebuff would disarm me.

Ilse smiled rather shyly and hung back. Maia, oddly enough, showed more pleasure. She grinned and gave a little bob, a sort of mock curtsy. I inclined my head in response. Randers gazed dolefully out of the window. Bland clapped his hands for the steward, who was obviously expecting him. He had put on a clean white jacket and carried a fresh tablecloth.

'I think there, by Mr Gregg, so that he may take part,' Bland directed.

The steward cleared the table nearest to Gregg and spread the cloth on it.

'The flags.'

The steward went to a cupboard and produced a collection of the little chrome flagstaff's with which Norwegians love to dress their tables. Some had pennants, some were bare. There were more pennants in a bundle.

'We will have as many countries as we can,' said Bland, but certainly we must have Norway — and England — and West Germany. Is there East Germany there also? Never mind. And, of course, Finland.' He laid a hand on Maia's shoulder. 'No, not the United States, please. She is not of Europe.'

The steward set out five little flagstaff's in a row. There was the Union Jack, the red and white Norwegian, the black and red and yellow West German, the blue and yellow Finnish, and finally the French tricolour.

'Excellent,' said Bland. He rearranged them so that the Norwegian flag was in the middle. 'Now, please, when I clap my hands, the other things I have asked for.'

The steward bowed out. I waited, fascinated, to see what came next. Bland held the stage.

'If we may wait just another little minute — ah, yes.'

The captain and the radio officer entered. They were wearing their best uniforms though the radio officer's shoes were still brown. Bland welcomed them.

'Herr Deputy Inspector, Herr Captain, young ladies, gentlemen, I must not bore you with a long speech — especially as I must say everything twice. I am only sorry my command of your own language, Herr Deputy Inspector, is not enough to do it justice.' This in English. He followed with a brisk sentence in what was evidently Finnish, turning to the girls.

I was distressed by the obedience of Maia's expression. I had a vision of her as Most Popular Girl and *victrix ludorum* of a county town high school. She watched Bland as if she had identified herself unquestioningly with his cause.

Bland reverted to English. 'You have all heard of the Spartapol scheme which I have been given the honour of organizing. Negotiations have been going on for some time to secure some land in Krossfjorden for our camp. I have heard by wireless that final approval may be expected tomorrow...'

There was a polite murmur from the assembly.

Bland acknowledged it with a little smile. 'Of course the actual transference of deeds and so on will take longer, and must be done by lawyers in dark offices many hundreds of miles from here. But I felt some small ceremony to mark the birth of the Spartapol ideal would be fitting on the spot, so to speak. That is why I have asked you here.'

He spoke again in Finnish, then beckoned to Randers. Randers handed him a large sheet of paper. Bland held it up.

'We call this our Spartapol Charter. It is not elaborately drawn, I'm afraid. We have only prepared it hastily this morning. Nor can it have any legal significance. But I think that we in the Spartapol movement will treasure it in years to come as a symbol of our first planting in these high latitudes. It is in German now — I think we must have it put into Greek as being more appropriate to our name! I will read it now in English. He cleared his throat. "To commemorate the founding of the first Spartapol camp in West Spitsbergen" — should we have others — "where the Youth of Europa may seek adventure, learn firmness and be imbued with a new spirit." Then the date, and "Aboard the D/S *Bellsund*, Ny Alesund," etcetera.

He looked up, the green-tinted spectacles glancing round the saloon. Another murmur of approbation. I watched Maia as the Finnish version followed. Her little face went stern, her little mouth tightened. She held her head higher.

'Now,' said Bland. 'I would like someone to sign our charter from each country represented here today. For Norway — would you honour us, Herr Deputy Inspector? You are kind. Will you please sit behind the table there? — so. For Germany I can sign. For Great Britain — Mr Panton, you have taken a great interest in our plans. Will you sign for your great country?'

I shook my head.

'Very well. Mr Gregg, you will —? Thank you. If you could just move a little nearer the table…'

The radio officer helped Gregg ease along the seat and propped him anew with the pillows.

'Lastly, Finland. I will not ask the little Miss Pori, for I wish her to sign on behalf of all Youth — she is our mascot already! Perhaps the other young miss would represent her beautiful land.'

Use had been hovering on the fringe of the assembly. She started when she realized Bland was addressing her, and took a pace forward. *You too*, I thought. Then she hesitated and looked in my direction. Suddenly I knew I had a chance of a small victory. It would make no difference in the long run, but I wanted it more than anything else in the world. Bland waited with his terrible composure. The invitation, vibrated in the air. Ilse took another step forward as the radio officer moved aside from her path, but she kept her eyes on me. *Don't do it*, I willed; *please don't do it*. She hesitated again. There was a silence as if everyone sensed the conflict. Ilse began to redden. Maia stared at her with set, angry face.

'Bitte.' Bland spoke at last. Ilse bit her lip and looked at the floor and said something with a nervous giggle, as if she were overcome with shyness. But she didn't move again, and I could have hugged her and yelled hallelujahs of encouragement. It was victory for sex and softness and civilization, defeat for regimentation.

Bland frowned. 'As you please. Miss Pori can sign for Finland additionally.' He called her in Finnish.

Maia stepped forward. She had slipped on the Spartapol sash I'd seen in the photographs. It was black with gold lettering. Now she added a little circlet of flowers twined round a headband. There was a ripple of approval from the saloon and someone clapped.

'Excellent,' cried Bland. 'How sweet our mascot is! You must sit right in the centre here.'

Maia slithered past them and took the centre place. She was flushed and smiling. My victory was already fading. I knew I must intervene, but I kept putting off the moment. I could guess the awful hush that would fall. I knew that my voice would go remote and flat and that I would put things badly and hesitantly.

Bland said, 'Now we must all sign the charter. First Mr Gregg. You are ready, Randers?'

Randers was. He had the Rollei with flash-gun fitted. *Blip* as Gregg signed. *Blip* as the deputy inspector signed. *Blip* as Maia signed, tip of pink tongue at the corner of the mouth. *Blip* as Bland signed, with quick decisive strokes. I drew breath and nerved myself to utter.

Bland clapped his hands and cried, 'Now everyone will drink a toast to Spartapol.'

Smartly on the cue the steward came in with a magnum of champagne, behind him the waitress who helped at mealtimes. She carried a tray of fluted glasses. The cork popped extravagantly and the assembly cooed in wonder. The timing was perfect. I'd lost my chance.

'Quickly, a glass for everyone,' said Bland. He caught sight of the Swedish tourist who stood at the door agape. 'Come in, dear fellow. Everyone welcome. We drink to Spartapol.'

The waitress was offering me a glass. I pushed it away.

Bland stood up. The rest of the table party, save Gregg, rose after him. Bland raised his glass, then noticed Gregg. He sat down again. 'We must not stand while Mr Gregg may not. Let us drink our toast seated, like officers in the British Navy.' He raised his glass a second time. 'To Spartapol, our fountain in the North!'

'Spartapol,' echoed everyone.

Bland noticed I was empty-handed. 'Mr Panton, you are not drinking? I thought you like drink.'

'I hate champagne,' I said. 'It makes me sick. Randers could have told you that.'

There was an uncomfortable silence. I found myself moving closer to Ilse and wishing I could hold her hand.

'Then you must have something different to drink — whisky or schnapps. Ask the steward directly.'

'It's all right. I don't require anything.'

'But the toast —'

'I wouldn't drink to Spartapol if I were dying of thirst. To hell with it.' The silence solidified. I could feel every pair of eyes in the saloon, even the steward's. I had to keep going at all costs. I fixed my eyes on Gregg and blundered on. 'I think the whole thing is wrong and corrupt. It may start off as a youth camp or whatever it is, which is bad enough anyway…' I could hear my voice droning away off the top of my head. 'I mean, all these things like cadet forces and sea schools and the Young Communists — or the Young Conservatives for that matter — are conformity things. If everyone goes dashing into the sea at five in the morning with glad cries it's a brave kid who says he'd rather stay in bed and think about girls. From doing alike to thinking alike is a short step.'

'Sparta will be only for those who *want* to attend,' said Bland, off balance. 'Not for weaklings.'

'I was coming to that. It seems to me you want to create some sort of élite. Well, I'm anti-élite. Wherever there's strong-arm stuff going in the world you can be sure there's an élite behind it. Parachutists, Commandos, shock-troops — the bloody old S.S.' I felt for the badge in my pocket. 'Talking of which…' I pulled out the badge and lobbed it on to the table. It landed amid the champagne glasses with a tiny clatter and lay there. Everyone stared.

'I found that,' I said, 'in the mine.'

Slowly, deliberately, Bland felt in his pocket. Another little emblem tinkled down. Poker-faced, he looked up at Randers. Randers obediently produced yet a third. Bland's was a *Stahlhelm* wound badge. Randers's was so old and discoloured it was hardly recognizable. It might have been some kind of sharpshooter's insignia.

'We have also found our souvenirs,' said Bland drily. 'There was a German weather station there during the last part of the war.'

'Manned by S.S. troops?'

'Who knows? By all sorts. Such detachments were often made up from the wounded and unfit.'

It was as if an asbestos shutter were being wound down inside my head. Suddenly I couldn't think of an answer. I opened and closed my mouth like a fish. Everyone looked hostile and uncomprehending.

The captain was the first to make a move. He set down his glass and wiped the back of his hand across his mouth and made a little bow to Bland. Thank you, but he must get back to work. The radio officer followed, though regretfully. The deputy inspector rose. I looked at Maia. Her little face was puzzled, but her eyes held no friendliness for me. Somehow I had spoilt her moment of glory. I picked up the S.S. badge.

'Surely you could have waited until the ship's officers had gone before coming out with that kind of stuff,' hissed Gregg.

I turned and faced Randers, but without seeing him really. Perhaps if I had looked into those evasive brown eyes I would have seen the terrible distress that must have been gathering… But I didn't. I just gave him the badge and said, 'You'd better have this. You've earned it,' and went out.

CHAPTER FORTY-ONE

Ilse followed me out of the saloon. I grabbed her hand and pulled her roughly along to my cabin. It was empty. Randers's belongings had gone. I kicked the door shut and grabbed her. 'What is the matter, Colin? What happened? What did you mean?'

'Nothing,' I said. 'Nothing's the matter. It's over now. They won. But at least they didn't get you and I love you. I love you!' I reached out and slid the bolt on the door. 'Let's make love.' I jerked at the zip on her slacks.

'No, not now.' She rescued her pants and unbolted the door, in that order.

I slumped on the bunk. I was tired, beaten. She hovered over me, eyes brimming with concern. Her hand was on my brow. It was nice.

'You are not well, Colin? What is the matter?'

'Nothing. Just tired, that's all. Must sleep.'

'Yes, sleep.'

'You sleep with me.'

She shook her head.

I let my eyes close and started to fumble ineffectually with my shirt buttons. After a moment I felt Ilse's hand take over. She got the shirt off, and my vest. Her lips brushed my chest in a fugitive kiss. She unbuckled my slacks. In a drowsy, passive way it was a feeling of utter luxury. I had an idea of what it was to be a girl, nicely seduced. Randers couldn't have come in at a worse moment. He banged on the door and entered almost simultaneously. The look on his face was of shock and unbelief. Then the door slammed shut again.

Ilse had gone scarlet. She started to cry. 'Oh Colin, what will he think?'

'I don't care what he thinks. But you'd better go, I suppose.' It was her fault for unbolting the door. 'I'll see you later. Don't worry.'

'I *cannot* go out now. He will be there.'

'No, he's going over to Krossfjorden again if I know anything about it. He probably came to say goodbye.' Poor old Randers. He was the easily shocked kind.

Ilse stood biting her lip.

I said, 'I'm sorry. It was my fault.' I wished she'd go now. She went without saying another word.

I'd automatically covered myself with the eiderdown. I pulled it right up over my head and stretched my toes and sighed. It was awful not to care but I really didn't. Everything was so bloody inconclusive and hopeless and I was in a soft white bed. And as I hovered on the brink of sleep I was vouchsafed — too late — the flashback I had wanted, a sudden sharp memory of a shiny coat under a lowering sky.

It was 1945 again, in a wet field by the side of a canal in Mecklenburg. The sky was grey and the rain dripped down so weakly that it scarcely pitted the canal surface. The big war had finally wound down the day before, but the things hadn't been signed yet. It was the pause between war and peace, the moment of anticlimax when the old soldier wondered if it was really all over and the young soldier wondered if he had qualified for a campaign star. I was the young soldier.

We had been well in the van of the armies in the last advance, which hadn't mattered in the least for there had been no serious opposition. Now we paused, under the rain clouds on a Mecklenburg farm. We slept in a stable, bedding rolls and looted mattresses spread on the straw, a container of thick tea curdling in the corner. The farmer's horses had been killed or stolen; a stained colour print of some former champion stallion was nailed on the wall behind me, some old bits of harness alongside.

For the moment we had no duties to speak of, and much of the day was passed in private and desultory patrols of the canal bank. Loot was the objective, loot was everyone's obsession. The countryside was poor in habitation but there was a swelling tide of refugees trying to escape the Russian advance. They came in ones and twos, in small parties, in whole families; some weighed down with packs and suitcases, others wheeling handcarts or loaded bicycles; Germans, Poles, Frenchmen, Belgians; plodding blindly westward in a trickle that was soon to become a flood.

They had to cross the canal and would come squelching through our fields looking for lock gates or a footbridge. Intermittently we stopped and questioned and even searched them. Sometimes they had been stopped before. They produced 'passes' written by recent investigators in exchange for confiscated goods. Certified free to travel, signed J. Ross, L/Cpl. Authorized to take a No. 14 bus to Piccadilly and there have a crap, signed B. L. Montgomery Field-Marshal. Bearer stopped and examined at Calbe, he had a liker, he doesn't now. Charlie-boy.

I was with a man called Saunders who was as near a chum as ever I acquired in my army career, and a little lance-corporal whose name I can't remember. The three of us had been out looking for eggs. You were allowed to buy them for German money. In the cookhouse they heated enormous pans of fat over the petrol burners and you took your own eggs along and fried them and clamped them between two hunks of bread and marge. I'm not sure if we had been successful this time. I think not.

Then we had stopped for a while out of earshot of the company to fire a little 6-mm. Browning automatic that the lance-jack had acquired. There was a small-arms craze going on. Saunders had a Walther with which he subsequently shot off the tip of his little finger. This little Browning was like a toy. We put up a tin at twenty yards. No one hit it. We closed in to five yards in the end and Saunders hit it once, then the ammunition ran out. We moved on.

On the canal towpath we came across a party of refugees. A man, a woman, and a girl of about fifteen. The man was wheeling a large suitcase on an old bicycle. The lance-jack stopped them, in his heavy way, with his few execrable words of German. Vo gayan see hin? Vo gayan see hin? The man muttered something and began to off-load the suitcase. I was suddenly bored and angered by it all.

The lance-jack's coarse red face was pushed expectantly forward. His G.S. cap was sodden with the rain and greasy at the rim. There was half a cigarette behind his ear. Saunders stood a little aside in his long dripping gas-cape, an officious expression on his face. He could be officious.

I said, 'Let's go, for Christ's sake.'

Saunders made to move.

'No, better hang on,' said the lance-jack to him.

I waited for a minute, staring across the canal to show my disinterest, then moved on. I must have covered a hundred yards when I saw the man in the black coat. He just appeared somehow. Perhaps he had been screened by a clump of trees. He came walking very quickly and purposefully towards the lock gates nearest the billets. Another man followed a pace or two behind, a tall gaunt man bowed down by a huge pack who looked as if he might be some sort of servant — almost a bearer. The man in the black coat carried only a stout leather briefcase.

In a moment they would pass me. I had one of my usual moments of indecision, then said '*Stop*,' rather nervously, and unslung my rifle. It wouldn't have been much use at close range and in any case it wasn't loaded. The others were still three hundred yards away.

The first man stopped at once and frowned. The other stopped a pace behind. He was bent and weary and looked down at his feet resignedly. The man in the black coat said something in a language which I didn't recognize, then a few words in German, which I recognized but at that time didn't understand. The coat was long and shiny and buttoned to the neck. He wore a beret on his head and — I happened to notice — galoshes on his shoes.

'Papieren,' I said. 'Papieren. Papers. Have you papers?'

The man frowned and fumbled under the flap of the coat. He brought out a pocketbook, opened it, and handed it to me. It was, I suppose, the first passport I had ever seen, and it was a Swedish one. I tried to turn over the pages, but it was awkward with only one hand. I had my rifle in the other. I was very conscious of the man's eyes on me. I handed him back the passport. He opened it at another page and shook out a typewritten slip stamped with endorsements in many colours and a white card embossed with a red cross.

'Red Cross,' he said in English. 'Sweden.' They were the only words he spoke.

I nodded and he put the documents away. I pointed at the briefcase.

'Was haben-sie da?'

He grew angry. His eyes hardened and his hand jerked open the buttons of the coat and thrust into his trousers pocket. For a fraction of a second I thought he might be about to draw a revolver or something. But he was only in search of a key.

I was suddenly fed up with it all again. I waved a hand and said, 'Okay, ist gut. Macht nichts.'

Black-coat looked at me questioningly a moment, then put the key back in his pocket and buttoned up. I looked wistfully at the briefcase. I had a vision of a beautiful Contax hidden away inside.

'Kein apparat? Binokular?'

Black-coat shook his head. The other man, who had been standing patiently, bowed, hitched up the huge pack on his back. I watched them cross the lock gates and walk steadily away.

Saunders and the lance-corporal came up.

'Who were they?' they asked.

'Just a couple of blokes.'

Saunders said, 'Get anything?'

'Sweet F.A. Did you?'

'No.'

The lance-jack said, 'The geezer in the black mac looked somebody. I bet he was a Nazi bastard.'

I said, 'No, he was Swedish. Swedish Red Cross. Just my luck.'

'How d'you know he was what he said? Bet he was a Nazi bastard.'

'I saw his papers.' But I felt a bit uneasy about it, inside.

Later I read in a week-old newspaper about Seidel, the Nazi philosopher, who had disappeared. He hadn't been well known to the general public. In fact I'd scarcely heard of him until then. But apparently Intelligence had been keen to have him.

They'd had a tip that Seidel was in the Lubeck area, trying to escape to the West with forged papers. I felt overwhelmed with guilt, though there was nothing specific to connect the man I'd let pass with Seidel. There must have been thousands of important looking people on the move. When I got home on leave a couple of months later I looked him up in the local library, in one of those books rushed out by patriotic publishers about 1941. This one had been edited by a major-general and introduced by a militant don and was called *Know your Enemies: The Nazi Leaders in Words and Pictures.* The picture of Seidel must have been an old one. It showed him in academic dress, presumably when he was still a lecturer at Cologne. Hair brushed back from his brow. He could have been the man in the shiny black raincoat, but it wasn't conclusive. I felt better. I read the piece alongside. Seidel had been an academic student until 1933. Biology. Then he'd written a book in defence of student duelling, and another rationalizing Nazism. He took a sabbatical year from the university, and as things turned out, never went back. In 1935 he turned up as cultural attaché at the German embassy in Madrid, later in Rome, finally Stockholm.

In 1939 he was back in the Fatherland, lecturing and running a special Party department. His province was youth, especially academic youth. I don't know if you could have such a thing as a Nazi intellectual, but if there were any it was Seidel's job to steer them from Hitler Youth through the temptations of university life and foreign travel without loss of faith. He also blossomed out as a poet and mystic. He was a great one for Destiny and the Splendour of Youth. He wrote poems in which the hero tousled the heroine in a cornfield, and then went off to war for his Leader and was killed, but the child lived on in the girl's womb, etcetera, and in the last stanza was dedicated to the Leader. In 1939 he was a war correspondent, heroic-poetic division, and wrote a rather nasty piece about dropping bombs on Warsaw. After that the book had no further news of him.

When I got back from leave the name of Seidel was already dropping out of currency. He hadn't been rated a very big fish, and he hadn't done anything very horrific as far as was known. According to the rumours he was in Russia or Spain or South America, but then so was Hitler himself. If the memory of that canalside encounter remained vivid in my mind it recurred less and less frequently. What had brought it flooding back now? Lying on my bunk, sinking in and out of sleep, I worked it out. It had been the way the Hermit hung back to the rear of Bland as we walked back to the water's edge from the Spartapol site. The old man was the link. Ten years earlier he had followed the man in the shiny black raincoat in just the same way. He was the same old man.

CHAPTER FORTY-TWO

I never heard the plane arrive, unless the sound of the motors got into a dream I vaguely recall, something to do with watching a motor race. A tap-tapping at the door woke me. I was still struggling to place what it was when it stopped and the door opened.

'Mr Panton, you are there?'

I blinked. I wasn't quite back in the world yet.

'It is me, the radio officer, Mr Panton.'

So it was.

'Oh yes,' I said. 'I was just coming to see you about changing duties tonight.' I said it very carefully, like you do when you're waking up.

He looked puzzled. 'What duties?'

I worked back over what I'd said. It must have been a fag end from another dream. 'I'm sorry. I got mixed up. What's happening. What time is it?'

I propped myself up and focused on my watch. It was nearly five. Five p.m., that must be.

The radio officer was looking at his, too. 'It will be five soon. There is someone asking to see you ashore. I guess he just arrived on the seaplane.'

'Oh,' I said. 'I didn't know there had been a seaplane. I'd better come.' I pushed a bare leg out of bed.

'I will wait outside,' said the radio officer hurriedly.

I found I was stiff and sore but otherwise remarkably well. Daytime sleeps are usually killers but apart from a dry mouth I felt fine. I splashed my face under the cold tap and swallowed a few mouthfuls, pulled on my clothes, and went into the corridor. The radio officer led the way ashore. We didn't encounter anyone on the way. I looked around as we walked along the landing stage. A hundred yards out in the fjord floated a Catalina flying boat. It was certainly a coming-and-going day for Ny Alesund.

I was pretty certain who the visitor was. I felt an up-bump of renewed optimism, then a down-bump of foreboding. There had been a lot of peace in mentally packing the whole thing in. Now I'd have to unpack. We went into the timber house that had been suggested as an hotel. There was a room furnished with an office table, some filing cabinets, and an unlighted stove. Rogerson lolled massively in an old elbow-chair, one foot jacked up on the stove. He wore the short hairy coat he'd worn when we first met. With a tin hat he could have been the colonel in any trench warfare drama.

'Hi,' he said. 'How did you get on?'

The relief of seeing him was enormous, but the sense of failure overwhelming. 'Not too well,' I said. I looked at the radio officer. He retreated.

'Sorry about the cloak-and-dagger approach,' said Rogerson. 'I wasn't sure who was still around on the boat.'

'No one much, actually. Bland and Randers went over to Krossfjorden again, I think.'

'Well, how did you get on?'

'I failed, that's how I got on. The whole thing's signed and sealed, or will be tomorrow. I'm sorry. I just wasn't able to stop it…'

'What happened?'

'They fixed it all, that's what happened. With champagne and a nasty little ceremony and Gregg wouldn't listen to me.'

'Who's Gregg? Never mind. Did you get a look at the place, as I suggested?'

'Oh, sure, I got a look. I saw enough for anyone, I should have thought. Then these lights went out. Anyway they wouldn't listen to me. It was just a waste of time. It's no good — I've ballsed the whole thing up.'

'Steady on,' said Rogerson. 'Start at…'

'You should have got someone else. I wasn't cut out for this lark. It's just been a balls-up from start to finish.' I struggled with a silly kind of sob that wanted to well up. I could feel my chin beginning to quiver. 'Honestly, in every way. I even poked the wrong girl.'

Rogerson laughed. His eyes were friendlier. 'If you've got all that off your chest, start at the beginning and tell me exactly what happened.'

'All right,' I said. 'Sorry.'

'Including about the girls.'

I told him, fairly well, only having to go back a couple of times with an 'Oh, I should have told you.' He interrupted twice with questions, the sort that go straight for the thing you've tried to gloss over.

'Did you actually look inside the coffin?'

'Well, no. The lid was fastened…'

'You didn't get right to the end of the mine shaft, then?'

'No.'

At the end he got up and paced the room once. 'All right, those are the observable facts. Now what do you suggest is the explanation? Tell me as if I didn't know anything. As if — as if you were outlining a story to a producer, someone like in your own line.' I suppose it comes instinctively to Nature's commanding officers to treat people like that

I said, 'Well, Bland is the practical man: scientist, meteorologist, expert in the Ionosphere, that kind of thing; in charge of the weather service in this part of the world for a while during the war; may even have been in Spitsbergen; would certainly know about the weather stations, one of which was — well, the one I've just been telling you about. It's also said he was involved in the rocket business, but I haven't been able to check that.'

Rogerson cut in, 'It's true. He was. I've been doing a little research of my own, with some — er — semi-official help. He went to America with von Braun and the rest but there wasn't much in his particular line the Americans didn't know already. He returned to Germany at his own request quite soon — about 1948 — to take up teaching. He'd been a Party man, by the way, but there was nothing else against him.'

'Anyway,' I said, 'the other man, the Hermit, is the ideologist. The name Fieseler may be his real name, but I doubt if he's really a professor; that's just part of the bird-watcher identity he's fixed up for himself in order to be allowed to stay in Spitsbergen. All that I feel sure about him is that ten years ago he was tagging along — literally — behind a man called Seidel who was a very sinister little theorist.' I described the canal bank meeting.

Rogerson listened impassively to the account of my unmilitary behaviour, and grunted, 'I remember about Seidel. He disappeared for good, didn't he?'

'As far as I know. There were the usual rumours about Spain and South America. Fieseler may not have been anything more than his chauffeur or batman. Presumably he stayed behind — I don't know. What matters is that he and Bland are now in this thing together. What's more, I don't think they get on awfully well. I got the impression they're rather willy-nilly accomplices. Randers, of course, is just a hired hand.' I paused. The exposition was hard work, and some of the bits were only falling into place as I talked. 'I feel pretty sure it's something

232

that was set up during the war. In fact for a while I thought that Fieseler must have been skulking over there in the weather station ever since, and that the coffin was full of food and stuff; I was all set to denounce the plot to the Norwegians. Then it turned out that he was quite official. Of course, there might still be Someone Else in the mine…'

Rogerson said sharply, 'Is that what you suspect?'

'Not really. I should have thought survival would be impossible for one year, let alone ten.'

Rogerson nodded. I guessed I'd made the right answer. 'What *do* you think, then?'

'Well, there's either a practical motive or an ideological one. I thought at first it must be practical. Bland's a practical man. I even thought of rockets, though I didn't know then that Bland had ever had anything to do with rockets. But the Spartapol camp would hardly fit in with that sort of thing. I mean, why go out of your way to have the place overrun with boys and girls? Anyway it became obvious to me that Spartapol wasn't just a cover. Bland is much too wrapped up in the idea. Whatever is going on over there, it's part of the Spartapol scheme. And if you want me to hazard a guess, it's some kind of museum.'

'Museum of what?'

It sounded hysterical, but I forced myself to finish. 'Oh, of the old Master Race stuff. Perhaps even of Nazism in particular. But with an extension to the whole of Europe, not just Germany. They're thinking on a bigger scale now.'

Rogerson weighed it up. 'You could be right,' he said finally. 'And incidentally I think you've done pretty well. Now this thing can still be fixed quite easily at Old Boy level, if you know what I mean. It'll have to be fixed tactfully, of course. The Russians are difficult enough about Spitsbergen as it is.

Meanwhile I think it's up to us to make sure once and for all about that mine. You don't know anything about explosives, by any chance, do you?'

'Yes, actually I do. I was in the Engineers.'

'Splendid. It'll be another night up for you, I'm afraid.'

I sighed. 'That's the worst of the Midnight Sun. No one goes to bed.'

'You'll get used to it. I've got some things to organize. You'd better collect anything from the *Bellsund* you want. We ought to be able to get back to Longyear tomorrow in time to rejoin her, but get your tickets and toothbrush and things in case we don't. And let as few people as possible know you're leaving.'

'Okay.' I got up.

'Just a minute.' Rogerson had forgotten something. He said, 'I'm sorry, old chap, I've been blinding along assuming you'd help. But you don't have to. I mean, you've done a lot already … '

'No, I'd like to finish now.' It was true. Besides, there was something reassuring about slipping into subordinacy again, letting him take over. You always have to call in the Establishment, in the end.

But there was one thing I still didn't understand.

'What did I say or do to bring you racing up here? I didn't have much luck with people like Gregg.'

'I happened to know Harry Williams. Met him up here.'

'Oh, I see — he didn't die at all, or he died a long time ago, you mean?'

'No. He died three weeks ago, in Exaltation. That was genuine enough.'

'What then?'

Rogerson almost grinned, but not quite. 'He hated the Arctic with all his guts. He swore that as soon as he'd saved enough money he'd leave it and never come back. And, by God, he worked hard and swindled hard to make it.'

I said with sinking heart, 'Then who is it in the white coffin?' He shrugged but must have read my thoughts. 'By the way, I didn't pick up anything about your friend Dancer, but someone's working on it for me.'

For the second time in twenty-six hours I watched the *Bellsund* sail away and wondered academically if I would see her again. The radio officer was going to tell everyone I was still sleeping in my cabin. I doubted if it would deceive some. Ny Alesund's scanty population had turned out in force to see the ship off. They lined the landing stage and waved. I stood back from the window in the timber house and added a sentimental wave of my own. I could see Maia and Ilse together on the raised afterdeck, rather forlorn.

CHAPTER FORTY-THREE

Half an hour later the Catalina drew a long spreading vee on the waters of the fjord and lifted into the air. As the familiar old parasol silhouette banked to head north, Rogerson and I walked round to the radio station.

'Haven't seen one of those since *South Pacific*,' I said.

'The Norwegians find them useful still. They've got the range. Not supposed to land here without special permission, really. They'll have to go back as soon as they've done this little job for us.'

In the radio station Rogerson clapped an earphone to one ear and grunted into the microphone which the operator obligingly held up for him. With his massive head sunk into his upturned collar and his great shaggy eyebrows pointing up like horns he looked more bull-like than ever.

As he listened his frown deepened. Twice he muttered short sharp interrogations and once a longer instruction.

'That's rum,' he said finally. 'There's no sign of Bland and Company or their boat. They've been up and down Krossfjorden twice, and now they've made a low run past the mine. One small dinghy pulled up on shore by the old harbour, that's all.'

'Yes, that was there yesterday. I had a nap in it. Bland's got the hire of a motorboat, about sixteen or twenty foot. Decked over, with two cockpits. Painted light blue, fairly shabby.'

Rogerson nodded. 'Well, there's nothing there now. They're going to come back round the point and see if there's anything on the way.'

I wandered outside and looked down the fjord. The Catalina showed up already, all wing and no body, like a foot-rule in the sky. The sound of the engines grew in volume and a couple of minutes later she rumbled over with a dip-in salute and turned out to sea again, this time heading for south and home.

Rogerson clumped out of the radio station. 'Looks as if they've skipped,' he said. 'Maybe the flying boat scared them when we arrived. They must have seen or heard it.'

'But they were so confident. Surely they wouldn't pack up just because a plane flew over. How were they to know it wasn't just a routine flight?'

'Bland knows this part of the world by now, Fieseler too — or whoever he is.'

'I can't see it. If they were alarmed the obvious thing would be to shove everything in the mine, drop a bit of roof, and play innocent. Anyway, what about all their things here in Ny Alesund?'

'Perhaps you're right. The point is that they're not there now. You can't hide a sixteen-foot motorboat just like that.' He looked at his watch. 'We might as well get going without further ado.'

Everywhere in Ny Alesund there seemed to be someone Rogerson knew, waiting to help him. Now it was the maintenance engineer from the mines, the one who'd been at the funeral. Jingling a bunch of keys, he led the way to the waterside railhead. A little black engine was wheezing expectantly.

'You mean we get a ride on this?'

'Sure,' said Rogerson benevolently.

We clambered aboard the solitary flat-truck coupled to the engine. The maintenance man gave a signal to the driver and we were off, puffing black smoke and accelerating to a madcap fifteen miles an hour. The sensation was enchanting, a kind of throwback to boyhood innocence.

At the other end of the line we walked past the deserted mine installations to the lone red-doored hut. The maintenance man unfastened the padlock and we squeezed in.

'What do you need?' asked Rogerson.

'Dunno. Anything would do, really.'

I was looking for the ammonal, which comes in big drums and is therefore distinctive.

'It's not a great blaster, but it sort of puffs things out very well,' I told Rogerson.

There didn't seem to be any, however. Mostly there were wooden boxes like ammunition boxes, short and square with rope handles at the end and stencilled letters on the side. One was open. Inside were cardboard boxes. Inside those were wrapped, rolled sticks the shape of half a pound of Co-op butter, only smaller.

'This'll do,' I told Rogerson. 'It's some brand of plastic explosive. Probably Polar-808. It'll do fine.'

'How much will you need?'

I tried to estimate. There were about eighty cartridges to a box and three boxes to a wooden case. Say sixty pounds of explosive per case.

'Four should do,' I said. 'Five to be on the safe side.' It was only a guess.

Rogerson and the maintenance man began to drag the cases out. What else? There was a nice big reel of primacord detonating fuse. I rolled it out. Primers, I'd need primers. I found a flat black tin like a paintbox neatly packed with 1cm. primers, the ones that look a bit like rifle blanks. Slow-burning fuse; there was some in a round japanned tin. At least, I hoped it was slow-burning. I tried hard to recall forgotten army expertise. Black had been the service colour for slow-burning, and orange for instantaneous. But hadn't civilians a different code? And anyway this was foreign. It was dark blue, nearly black, and it looked all right. There was a complete roll of the stuff, the ends still waxed over, and an odd length three or four yards long. I took the odd length and gave it to Rogerson.

'Ask the man if it's slow-burning, would you?'

He came back in a second. 'He seems to think so.'

The detonators were stored separately, in a bricked-off cubbyhole by the door: little aluminium cylinders about two inches long, open at one end, closed at the other. I took a couple and put them with the cigarettes in a twenty-packet I was carrying. There was one other thing.

'Must have some Sellotape or insulating tape,' I told Rogerson. 'And something to cut it.'

'I've got a penknife. I'll ask about the tape.'

The maintenance man nodded and pointed back to the main mine-working. We carted the stuff along and loaded it on to the truck. The maintenance man peeled off into another store and came back with a roll of insulating tape. Back at the landing stage we off-loaded the five cases, the reel, the tin of primers and the length of slow fuse, and lowered it all into a boat. It wasn't much of a boat, an old open affair like a ship's lifeboat with the engine in a sort of dog kennel amidships.

'Best I could do,' said Rogerson briefly. He eyed the handsome bulk of the Governor's launch regretfully. 'At this stage we mustn't involve the authorities any more than I have already. If by any chance you're wrong, young Panton, there'll be trouble enough as it is.' He looked back at our boat. 'But the boatman's a good chap.'

He certainly looked reassuring: a big scrubby blond man with sleeves pushed back from gnarled forearms.

The maintenance man had been busy drawing up a painstaking receipt in a notebook. He proffered it to Rogerson, who dipped into an inside pocket and produced a gold fountain pen to sign it. Like I said, you can't do without the Establishment in the long run.

'Tak.' The maintenance man pocketed his book and trudged away without looking back. It was getting on for nine o'clock.

CHAPTER FORTY-FOUR

The journey across was uneventful, almost unreal. Clouds covered the sky and blanked out the top of Grimaldi. A misty rain settled rather than fell. Time had that curious suspended quality again.

The old tub wasn't fast. It was nearly half past eleven as she rumbled alongside the ruined jetty of Holyroodhamna. There was no sign of Bland and Co. The ancient punt hadn't moved. Rogerson heaved himself ashore, keeping his right hand in his pocket as if he held a gun there. I remember wondering if people did this because they'd seen it on the pictures. Or was it an instinctive man-of-action gesture? I pointed out the mine and the distant weather station or Hermit's Abode.

'We could really do with an extra hand,' said Rogerson. 'Someone to take a walk along there and have a look-see. I hadn't realized everything was dispersed quite so widely. It'll be an awful waste of time if we all have to go.'

'We could keep an eye on it from the mine, couldn't we? Without bothering to go along.'

'I'm sorry. I wouldn't feel safe. We'll just have to have a quick look first. We can recce the winding house at the same time.'

'Okay.' I was thinking about those five heavy cases of high explosive. Sooner or later they'd have to be hauled up to the mine. I said, 'It seems silly to go up empty-handed. Perhaps we should take something with us.'

'Good idea.'

We decided on a light load for this preliminary expedition: a single case. We took a rope handle each, Rogerson the lefthand one, so that he could keep his right hand in his pocket. The boatman stayed with the boat.

It was a tedious climb. After five minutes I was longing to change arms. Half-way up we let the case down for a breather.

'This is where Bland made his speech,' I said. 'The one about the fountain of youth and all that.'

'Uh-huh.' I was glad to notice he was a little out of breath.

As we approached the winding house we instinctively moved more quietly, more slowly. Twenty yards away Rogerson motioned to put the case down again. He went on alone and entered. I followed. It was unchanged.

'Doesn't look as if anyone's here.' I heard my voice echoing dully.

Rogerson had produced a torch and was shining the beam into the mouth of the mine. 'You went down there?' he said. 'It must have taken a lot of guts.'

'I surprised myself. Actually, it was better with the lights on. As the bishop said to the actress.'

I poked round behind the rubble in the corner and uncovered the little generator again. I unscrewed the tap and peered into the tank. It seemed to be empty still.

'We need some petrol. I forgot.'

Rogerson switched the torch off. 'There's a can in the boat. Look, I've decided. I'll pop along to the weather station and see if anyone's there. You can go back to the boat and fetch the petrol.'

'All right.'

'You might as well bring the boatman, too. His name's Odd by the way.'

'You can say that again.'

Odd hadn't been idle. He'd unloaded the stuff and stacked it ashore. He got the purport of my signs cheerfully enough, rummaged in his boat for a gallon can of petrol and pointed inquiringly at the boxes of explosive. I nodded and he swung a case effortlessly on to his back. I settled for the petrol, the primacord and the odds and ends. Well someone had to take them. Anyway by the time we reached the top again both arms were ready to drop off. The reel of primacord wasn't anything like the weight of a case of H.E. — twenty pounds, perhaps. But the thick drum shape was about as awkward for one-arm carrying as a spare wheel.

I'd been watching the weather station anxiously whenever the contours of the hillside didn't hide it. Rogerson reached it when we were half-way up. Now he had just started on his way back, apparently unconcerned. That was a relief, anyway. I gave Odd a cigarette and we smoked in silence. He seemed totally incurious about the whole affair.

Rogerson made the universal nix sign as he approached, crossing and uncrossing his arms before him. 'No one there,' he reported. 'Otherwise just as you described it, including the books. I had a glance at them. They're not incriminating in themselves, really. I mean you can't hang a man for having *Scouting for Boys* — did you notice it?'

I shook my head.

'It was there. English edition, too. What else? Oh yes, the stove was cold. Can't have been a fire in the last twelve hours, I should say.'

'Looks as if you're right and they've skipped,' I said.

Rogerson stamped the snow from his feet. It was twelve thirty a.m. Time was passing much more quickly than the previous night.

He said, 'I think we'll take a look inside now. Odd can come with me if you've seen enough down there.'

'No, I'll come. He can keep cavey.'

We got the generator going and Rogerson led the way down the shaft, occasionally flashing his torch on the walls. There was no music. I sensed that he thought I'd imagined that bit. I counted the lights as we came to them. Eight, nine, ten, eleven. Any moment I expected to find the shaft sealed by a fall of rock.

Then the twelfth light gleamed minutely ahead. Under it stood the miner's bogie. But now the bogie was empty.

'Well, something is changed,' I whispered.

Rogerson was shining the torch systematically around. The rays confirmed what I had suspected. Just beyond the twelfth light the shaft proper came to an end. The two low tunnels that led off were primitive and uninviting. Rogerson turned the torch downwards. The smooth, hard floor showed markings as if something had been dragged into the right-hand tunnel. It must have been something heavy.

'The lighting cable goes that way, too,' I whispered.

Rogerson said, 'It looks as if we crawl from here.'

'Both of us?'

'It can't be much fun along there alone.'

'Equally it wouldn't be much fun leaving your way back unguarded. That's the way I feel about holes, anyway.'

'Um,' said Rogerson, reflectively.

'In a way I'd rather go alone, knowing you were here.'

'How do you know there isn't someone waiting?'

'If there is, he's old and infirm.'

'All right' said Rogerson. 'One goes. Toss you for it.'

We watched the 50-øre piece land on the floor and roll away into the shadows.

'I'll go,' I said decisively.

I took off the plastic mac. It would get in the way, and a tear down the back was already two feet long.

'Do you want the gun?' So he did have one.

'No thanks. Just the torch.'

Actually it wasn't necessary to crawl. Once under the first transom there was enough headroom to squirm along in a kind of bent-double Cossack-dance locomotion. The last faint light gleamed ahead now more distinct, more pinkish. The air seemed colder and drier than ever and the musty catacombs smell more acute. It was a squirm of perhaps fifty yards in all. Then suddenly I could stand up.

The light was raised high. The redness came not from the source itself but from the monstrous scarlet banner that hung on the wall behind. I had entered what must have been a natural chamber in the rock, tall and narrow and roughly triangular in shape. At head height the walls began to lean in, giving the impression of an arched roof as if it were a chapel or crypt. The floor was lost in shadow; there was only a suggestion of dark shapes, and one bright gleam from something like a piece of silver which reflected the light bulb above.

So far I hadn't switched on the torch, preferring to be part of the gloom rather than pierce it. Now I aimed straight ahead and held my breath and pressed the button beneath the rubber armour. In the sudden beam of light the polished thing was bright and pure, a sort of silver chalice. But the banner, where the direct rays struck it, showed faded and brown, the folds thickly crusted with dust, so that only now did I pick out the familiar crooked motif that sprawled across its centre.

I let the beam sink, and though I had been expecting what I saw in the immediate foreground the sight still gave me a start.

It was the White Coffin, hardly a couple of yards from where I stood. Almost subconsciously I noted the wooden rollers underneath it and ticked off the answer to the question, how had it been moved on through the low tunnel? The rest of my attention was already on the dark shapes just beyond the coffin. There were two of them, side by side at the foot of the banner, indistinct in the gloom but somehow sepulchral in their mere disposition. Between them the silver vessel stood on a square something — a box, perhaps — covered with a blanket. I heard my pulse beating in my head. I crept closer.

The figures rested on rough catafalques of rubble in the stiff attitude of death. As I bent over the first I clung to the wild hope that it might still be only a waxwork or effigy. It wasn't. I may have gasped out loud or I may only have thought the gasp, but certainly my stomach started to contract and the back of my mouth to dilate. Instinctively I jerked the torch beam aside and managed to fight back the sickness. It was the worst thing I'd ever seen, worse than the drowned sailor whose features had been eaten by fish, worse than the fading dismay on the face of the soldier who'd idly picked up a *panzerfaust* antitank charge and eviscerated himself.

What was left of the skin of the face was dark and mummified and peeling at the edges like a badly mounted painting. The fleshless nose jutted like a little parrot beak. Charred lips had receded from calcified teeth. But somehow the most dreadful thing of all was the hair — or rather the wig. The body was evidently of a woman — which woman I could already guess — and the revolting relic of a head had been pushed into the kind of sculpted wig you used to see in hairdressers' windows, tight little waves of enamelled blondness, not a hair out of line. It was several sizes too big, so that naked skull showed under the edges; and quite clearly it was of much later origin. It was dust-free and as new and bright as everything else was dead and decayed. I turned, quaking, to the other figure.

I suppose the petrol had done a pretty thorough job and someone had attempted an ambitious but inexpert reconstruction almost from scratch. In a way it was so man-made that it was easier to take. Over whatever had been left of the face had been sprayed some pink plastic stuff which reproduced the submerged contours in a blurred, flattened form; the nose scarcely obtruded at all, the eye sockets were mere depressions; of ears there was no sign; the whole lower jaw was revealed, where the plastic film had curled back, as a clumsy cement replacement. But a mouth had been marked out with lipstick and a chin defined. A lock of artificial hair and an artificial moustache completed the picture, a cartoon of the man as crude but unmistakable as the ones I had drawn in my school books fifteen or twenty years before.

The body of the woman was dressed in some dark garment buttoned high at the neck; of the man in a brown shirt and tie. Neither seemed to have any bulk. The clothes were sunken and shapeless, as if they were empty. Both trunks disappeared at the waist into folds of blanket which hung over the improvised biers. Both had arms folded rigidly across the breast, terminating — as a last macabre touch — in yellow kid gloves.

'Like Mickey Mouse,' I said busily to myself. 'Like Mickey Mouse and Minnie Mouse and Mickey Mouse and Minnie Mouse and Mickey Mouse and Minnie Mouse …'

I'd had enough. I started backing towards the tunnel. I felt the back of my leg just above the ankle catch against something but I couldn't save myself. Luckily I hadn't straightened up very much and I didn't fall heavily. I overcame a moment of panic and shone the torch on the obstruction. It was a record-player, one of those slick little battery-powered, transistorized ones; common enough in Germany at that time though not yet familiar in Britain. The records were on the ground behind it: quite a lot of Wagner, only to be expected; Weber; Greig; *Ein Heldenleben* — so they'd even embraced Strauss; Sibelius; and Berlioz's *Lélio*, or The Return to Life, as well as the *Symphonic Funèbre et Triomphale* in the coloured sleeve that had teased me half-way up Europe.

'Christ,' said Rogerson when I got back, 'you look as if you've seen a ghost.'

'I've seen worse. You'd better go and have a look too. I want someone else to have seen it.'

CHAPTER FORTY-FIVE

He came scuffling and squeezing back within fifteen minutes. All he said was, 'I'd never have believed it.'

'Did you see the hands? Like Mickey Mouse and Minnie Mouse.'

'Um. I took a peep in the white coffin, by the way.'

'I thought the lid was fastened.'

'Not anymore.'

'Who was it?'

'I'm not sure, except that it wasn't Harry Williams, the old crook.'

'What ought we to do about him?'

'Just leave him with the other two, and fix the lot of them, for all time. That's the main thing.'

'How do you suppose the first two got here? Do you think it was the U-Boat I dreamed up?'

'Very possibly.' He was short now, bemused I suppose by what he'd seen. 'There was some story of one slipping out of Lubeck round about May 1st or 2nd, but I don't see how the bodies could have been got out of Berlin. Anyway, they were supposed to have been burned up with petrol.'

'By the looks of things they were,' I said with a shudder.

We walked back in silence, trundling the empty bogie in front of us. It would do to carry the stuff into the mine.

If Odd noticed anything about us he didn't show it. We walked down to the water's edge again. Now there was the wearisome chore of getting the rest of the explosive half a mile uphill.

'If only we had a sledge we could drag it,' I said.

Rogerson scowled. 'They must have had something like. Didn't see it anywhere.' He swung one of the boxes on to his back. Odd picked up another, as effortlessly as before. I heaved at a third. It landed on my shoulder awkwardly, banging my ear. We set off.

It was a brute of a carry. Odd moved quickly into the lead, then Rogerson. I came third, but after about half way I ceased to care about the others. My whole concentration was on the slippery slope and the hard, unbalancing box on my back that dug into my neck and dragged at my arms. I got there finally.

'Break,' said Rogerson. 'We've earned it.' He hadn't long arrived himself. He was breathing very heavily and his face had gone dark red. A big fat vein on his temple was pulsing noticeably.

'I feel like a worker ant,' I said. 'Carting things around six times its own weight.'

Rogerson produced cigarettes. I wasn't sure if this was a good idea when so out of breath but I took one. Odd inhaled a couple of puffs of his and said something to Rogerson and set off downhill again.

'He's gone to fetch the last box,' said Rogerson.

'Hooray for him.'

We loaded the four cases we had already on to the bogie, piled the rest of the gear on top, and set off down the mineshaft again. I hadn't minded the previous exploration with Rogerson; this time I was uneasier.

Once or twice was all right. Three times was daring Fate to do something. At the end of the tracks, under the twelfth light, Rogerson said, 'What now?'

I took the torch from him and flashed it around. I wasn't awfully sure. 'Well, for a bursting charge you just put the stuff in the middle of the space and blow it. You get a terrific pressure, then a terrific vacuum. It's the vacuum that does the damage. The whole thing caves in.' I was feeling my way. 'But it's different for underground chambers.'

'I'm sure it is,' said Rogerson roughly. He didn't understand I was trying to talk myself into remembering.

I said, 'I think the best thing would be to give the roof a good clout. You know, jar it up a fraction of an inch so that it falls back and the whole lot comes down. Just back there would be a good spot.'

I'd noticed that about fifteen or twenty feet back the roof looked particularly insecure. The shoring was denser and stronger; there were two big beams within ten feet of each other, both stoutly supported at the ends. And the ceiling sloped to one side in a hard line, as if it were the edge of a massive slab of rock.

'Whatever you say.' He made me feel like an apprentice plumber sent up to the big house to fix a ballcock.

'The thing is, we need to wedge the stuff hard against the roof. Otherwise it won't work.'

'All right. You're in charge now.'

'The easiest way would be to take a chance and drop one or both of those big supports there, then use the timbers. The snag is that it might bring down a bit of roof prematurely.'

'Comes to the same thing in the end,' said Rogerson carelessly.

'Let's get cracking.'

We pushed the bogie back to the exit side of the weak spot. The props were the tree-trunk sort, tough and solid. Rogerson kicked one. It was wedged in tight.

'We need a sledge-hammer at least,' he said. He looked at our equipment moodily. 'Would that stuff go off if we used one of those boxes?'

'It's supposed to be pretty stable,' I said. 'But I wouldn't like to risk it. Cold temperatures are more dangerous.'

In the end we emptied a case, and filled it with rubble. As a battering ram the result was heavy enough but the shape was all wrong. The only way to wield it was for us to take a rope handle each and swing the thing end-on.

'Ready?' said Rogerson. 'One, two, *three*.'

Crash. I felt the rope twist and tighten on my hand. Nothing else happened. We tried again. There was a creaking from somewhere above. We were both jammed against the mine wall and I wondered hard if we'd be able to retreat fast enough when the beam came down.

'One, two, *three*.' The prop began to shift.

'This time,' said Rogerson.

Crash again. It began to topple towards me. I dropped my end of the explosives box and skipped away. Fractionally later the prop thumped down where I had been.

'That's the trouble with hitting them low,' said Rogerson. 'They fall towards you.'

The transom was sagging but still up, held by the tight pinning of the prop that other end. We shifted that one more easily but the beam caught Rogerson a clout on the side of the knee as it came down. He swore and hobbled about in pain. Eventually we had the whole lot down: two massive twelve-by-twelve beams and four props and a certain amount of dust and debris from above but no major land-shift. Rogerson was still panting; he'd supplied most of the brute force.

The next bit was tedious and involved emptying the other three cases of explosive. We ballasted them with more rubble and stood them in twos, end on, a pair on either side of the shaft. Now the task was to get the two beams up and across the gap, supported on our improvised piers. They were both heavy but the second one was the beast. I could hear Rogerson heaving and grunting and feel the strength of his back. When we finally got them in place he retreated a couple of yards and sat down.

'Are you all right?' I didn't like to shine the torch on him.

'Yes. Just a bit … winded. Be all right in a minute.' He spoke with a little difficulty. He was trying to breathe steadily, but short desperate gasps kept asserting themselves.

I turned back to the structure we'd made. With some diagonal pinning from the four props, which looked to be about the right length, it would be quite a steady job. There was a gap varying from six to twelve inches between the top of the beams and the roof. I started on the laborious business of unwrapping stick after stick of the explosive and packing it into the space. It was stiff and unyielding; a box lid served as a rammer. The stuff smelled strongly of marzipan and I remembered it was supposed to penetrate the skin of the hands and get into the bloodstream and give you a headache if you handled too much of it.

Looking back, it was curious how such matter-of-fact reflections had taken over. The monstrous secret of the Chamber of Horrors fifty yards away had fallen into acceptance as readily as the new film at the Odeon. But I was worried about Rogerson.

When his breathing sounded healthier I returned to him, letting the torchlight catch his face. He looked pale now, and glistening with sweat.

He said, 'Sorry to leave it all to you. I'm better now.'

'I can finish off on my own now, easily. It's straightforward from here.'

'No, don't be silly.' He started to get up, and winced. 'That beam gave my knee a fair old clout.'

'It's not only the knee, is it?'

'Well, the old heart's a bit dickery. But it often does that. Nothing to worry about. The doctor says I'm overweight.'

'You're going back out of here.'

'Nonsense.'

'Come on,' I said. 'I'd feel much easier if you were watching the rat-hole from the outside, and if Odd were watching the boat. The sooner we get away from this little fairy grotto the better.'

Rogerson stood up.

'Sit on the trolley.'

'Like hell. I can manage.'

But after a hundred yards he stopped and sat on the edge of the bogie for a rest. I gave it a push forward and he slid back, into it, feet off the ground. I kept on pushing and we carried on that way.

CHAPTER FORTY-SIX

In the daylight he looked distinctly grey, with little clusters of red veins showing brightly round his nose and cheeks. But the big thumping vein on the temple had subsided.

He sniffed the air and said, 'I'll be all right now. It was very close in there.'

'I know.' Actually it was deadly cold.

Odd had returned with the fifth and last crate. We sent him down again to the boat and Rogerson took up a position in the winding house that gave him a good view out.

'Right,' I said. 'Last reel. Won't be long.'

I set off down the shaft once more, pushing the bogie and the case of 808 in front of me. This was the fourth time, never mind the third, but I was engrossed by the job.

I finished placing the explosive much more quickly now, using unopened packets of the stuff and only unwrapping individual cartridges for squeezing into the final crevices. In the end it took the whole of four cases, or nearly 200 lb. If that didn't bring down a bit of mountainside I couldn't think what would. With a couple of the props wedged in diagonally underneath the beams, the charge was held pretty firmly against the roof, with no air space intervening. That was the art as far as I could remember. The question of what to do with the case of H.E. that was left over I deferred for the time being. Meanwhile there were trimmings to attend to.

I fished out Rogerson's penknife and cut off a couple of hefty lengths of primacord. The end fitted neatly into the open ends of the primers and there was a little sleeve you could pull down to hold them tight. I pushed the primers into the explosive, one at each end of the charge. In the gloom the primacord hung down like lengths of plastic clothes line. It's a detonating fuse: that is to say, it explodes rather than burns. It carries a shock wave along at tremendous speed — something like four miles a second — and is therefore useful for linking together a number of widely-spaced charges. But it needs a bit of a bang to get it going and sometimes it blows itself out in an excess of zeal. To make absolutely sure of a demolition you make an elaborate ringmain so that if the detonation wave fails in one direction it still goes whooping round in the other.

There wasn't time for that now. I gathered up the two loose ends of primacord and also the running end from the reel of the stuff and taped them all together for three feet. The last bit was simple. I remembered the drill as if it were only yesterday the Q.M.S.I. had been endlessly going over it in the lecture hut at Clitheroe. Cut off the first foot of safety fuse and throw it away, in case the damp had got in. I only had the one piece; I cut off a foot from both ends, leaving about ten or eleven feet. Slip a detonator over one end and crimp it tight. I felt among my cigarettes and picked out a detonator, carefully holding the open end. Didn't have a crimping tool but managed to crush the hollow end over the fuse by pinching it between the blade and body of the penknife. Slide the detonator into the neck of another 1cm. primer. Fix yet one more primer to the end of one of my primacord leads. Tape the two primers securely together.

I took the torch and had a closer look. For near-darkness it wasn't a bad job. I had a length of slow-burning fuse that would burn for about five or six minutes and then — well, with two leads to the charge, at least a ninety-nine per-cent certain bang. There was also the rest of the primacord, hundreds of feet of the stuff still wrapped on the drum. In this form it constituted a separate and highly mobile charge which would go off at the same time.

I sat back off my haunches and lit a cigarette. This was the last test, the final ordeal. It was perfectly obvious where the surplus charge should go. There had never been any doubt. It should go in the Chamber of Horrors right between — or better still *under* — Mickey and Minnie, and blow both obscene exhibits into tiny bits. The only drawback was that I didn't want to go into the Chamber of Horrors again. I'd never wanted to go anywhere less in my life.

I checked the time. Amazingly, it was after four in the morning: 4.06 to be exact. I closed my eyes and thought, at four ten I'll act. It was terribly important to do it if I could. But if I didn't no one would blame me. Rogerson hadn't even laid down that it ought to be done. If I went back now and we blew the charge the mine would probably be sealed for evermore. What remained inside it wouldn't matter. On the other hand had I not used the argument myself — to Gregg — that it might be ten or twenty years before anyone would want to open up the place? By sealing it off and leaving the nasty little waxworks intact we'd be preserving the possibility.

I reflected that I'd had quite a good life so far. I wasn't a success, certainly. But I'd never gone hungry. I'd had some fun, some pleasant drinking, a lot of good company, a little lechery and a taste of love. The bit of war I'd seen had hardly contained a shot fired in anger. I was unmarried. Thanks to a shrewd accountant I hadn't even paid much income tax. On the whole I'd got out rather more than I'd put in. It seemed that I owed civilization the effort.

I rolled the primacord drum through a gap in the scaffolding before me, shoved the case of explosive after it, and then crawled through. Getting on the wrong side of the charge wasn't very comforting in itself. There was still the pitch-black, cramped passage to negotiate.

I found the best way of progressing was to kneel behind the case, lift it by the two handles and shove it as far forward as I could with a wild, straining heave. It was slow and noisy but better than trying to slide it. Each throw knocked the primacord drum rolling on ahead, unwinding as it went. The main problem was what to do with the torch. In the end I abandoned all hope of keeping it on, and put it in my pocket.

Gradually the pinkish light got nearer. With a last convulsive effort I was in the crypt. I turned the case endways on and pushed and strained at it, past the white coffin, until it was between the two recumbent grotesques. I lifted one end and wedged the primacord reel underneath. There was still several hundred feet wound on. It would surely explode with enough force to detonate the caseful of explosive. I straightened up and took a peek at Mickey and Minnie. They hadn't moved. In a few minutes they'd be — well, dispersed. And not before time.

The enigma of the white coffin remained, a last mystery that I could solve. Rogerson had said the lid was now loose. I held the torch at the ready and lifted one edge. It was heavier than I'd expected. I pressed the torch button. The face was grey and — after the others — impersonal, neutral, harmless; like a solidified photograph. It was ten years since the canal bank incident and I had been brooding over-much lately about it: but I was fairly sure it was the same man. I let the lid fall again.

There was one last touch that seemed fitting. I switched on the little record player and groped for a record. It proved to be the Berlioz Symphonic. They didn't deserve that, but I was prepared to be magnanimous. Music for Exploding Lovers. I kept the volume down for fear of alarming Rogerson. I had blindly put on the second side, beginning with the slow trombone lament or Oraison. In the stillness the notes hung nakedly, plaintively. And as I listened to them I became aware that I was no longer alone.

CHAPTER FORTY-SEVEN

'Wer ist da?' The sound came from behind me. I jerked round.

The thing I saw first was a bayonet, gleaming where it caught the light. Behind that an old rifle. Behind that the old man, crouched in the shadows of the tunnel.

I said in German, 'Just a friend. A friend of Randers!'

He advanced slightly and stood higher. Old eyes stared at me from under the peak of his cap. But the bayonet was fairly steady and it was pointing at my middle. It was shiny though streaked with rust, as if it had been lying around for a long time and then roughly sharpened.

He said, 'Where are they, the others? Dr Bland? Randers?'

Where indeed? I thought for an instant. 'Did they not come to take you away?'

'No. What do you mean? I don't understand.'

'Then they've gone. They must have left you.'

'It is not true. Where are they?'

'They've gone. They should have come to tell you. The authorities are suspicious. We must seal off the mine with explosives for a while and come back later.'

The bayonet wavered, then straightened again. 'And Dr Bland and Randers agreed to this?'

'Naturally.'

'You lie. Randers knew nothing of this last place. He is a fool and a weak man and was never trusted. You are an enemy.'

'No, a friend.' My principal emotion was sheer resentment lest I be pipped at the post. If anything went wrong now it would be like getting killed on the last day of war. He must have been lurking in the other tunnel.

'What is all this?' He indicated the case of 808.

'Just some more things to be left here. Your books should come in as well…'

He took a step forward. The bayonet bobbed nearer. I couldn't help retreating, between the two catafalques. Another pace and I'd be hard up against the case of explosive.

'There's someone else outside,' I started to say. He must have been nerving himself for the lunge. It came. It was a clumsy one and I might have dodged it altogether if it hadn't been for the case of explosive. Raised up on top of the primacord drum it caught me just behind the knee. I started to trip and only saved myself by reaching wildly out. My hand struck something yielding and leathery. At the same time the rifle took me in the thigh, high up on the inside. It felt like a blow from a heavy stick. The back of my head hit the banner, and dust rained down. I was still thinking, *It's all right, it didn't go in, it must have been only the muzzle*, when suddenly there was blood trickling down my leg.

I felt the darkening, racing sensation of shock. There was something so crude and basic about a bayonet. But fear kept me going. I lurched to my feet, grabbing at the banner for support. It came billowing away from the rock face and the wooden stretcher clattered down across the rifle as the old man advanced for another poke at me. I grabbed the barrel and jerked it out of his hands. I swung wildly. The butt took him on the elbow with a dry brittle noise. He crumpled to his knees, holding the elbow tightly with his other hand. We breathed heavily at each other.

In the rays from the overhead light, clouds of dust settled slowly, vertically down to the floor. I became aware, as if across a great passage of time, of the trombone lament.

'What did you want to do that for?' I said.

He didn't reply. With a sudden movement I pulled the rifle back and reversed it, as quickly as I could in the cramped space. I jerked the bayonet in the direction of the exit tunnel. I wanted him to move. I wanted to get out of this terrible place. He stared back without moving. His peaked ski-cap had been dislodged sideways so that it tipped over one eye at a ludicrous rakish angle.

I inched forward and gestured again. 'Come on, move.'

No effect.

I decided to try another tack. 'We met once before, you know, many years since.' There was no response at first. I had a brainwave and added, 'All three of us. Seidel, too. He was there.'

In the poor light I could just see his eyes come alive again. I had touched his interest.

'It is Seidel, isn't it?' I indicated the white coffin.

'Yes.' His voice was only a whisper.

I said gently, 'Why him? He wasn't so … important.'

'It was his vision. He thought of it first.'

'He has come a long way to take his own place in it.'

'So.' He inclined his head, though whether out of agreement or respect for the dead I couldn't be sure.

'It was many years since you last saw him?'

'Yes.'

'You were his servant?'

'I was his teacher. He was my finest pupil. He was a great man. In the time of greatness, yes, I was proud to serve him as best I could.'

'The others,' I said. 'How did they get here?'

Tactically it was a mistake. Once off the subject of Seidel the old man froze again. 'Who are you? Why do you ask?'

'A friend. I told you. Tell me how Seidel began it.'

'It was in 1942, when it first seemed possible we might not win. Hess had just gone. Seidel believed that there might have to be another defeat before the Eternal Reich could become a reality.' He recited in a low monotone, as if it were something he had often rehearsed to himself. 'He also believed that there must be continuity, some flame to stay alight, some spring to keep flowing. He conceived Operation Last Resort to be put into operation should the worst befall our country. It was not official. It was worked out at a private dinner party in Berlin: only twelve people ever knew of it. I was one of the twelve. The Leader did not know of it himself, but near the end the commander of his bodyguard and his private pilot were consulted.'

'And Bland?'

'He too was not involved until near the end. He was in Lubeck and he knew the Arctic. Seidel thought that only the Arctic would now be suitable. Earlier it had been hoped that the Last Resort might be on German soil, hidden away. But that had become impossible. In the last days the two bodies were flown in the light plane from Berlin to Schwerin and then by car into Lubeck. The U-boat was waiting as it had waited for four weeks. In the night it put to sea. No more was heard of it, and for many months we feared it had been lost before its task was completed. But then Bland discovered that the Krossfjorden weather station had been deserted when the British arrived, and we were able to hope that perhaps our U-boat had reached its destination, and taken those men off, and had been lost only on the return journey. In 1950 I was able to come here the first time as an ornithologist. Last year we penetrated the obstruction in the mine the U-boat commander had made according to his instruction.'

'Seidel didn't go with the U-boat, then?'

'No. He escaped to Spain and then to South America. It was important that someone should survive who knew. There were three of us who did. Now there are two.' He looked up. 'And one of the two is not worthy.'

I bit back an interruption.

'He has no vision.' He was talking to himself as much as to me. 'He could never see the holiness and the beauty of this shrine. He thinks only of how many young people — pilgrims I would have them called — he can bring at a time and what they will eat and how they will arrive and what exercises they will do. He has the mind of a drill-sergeant.'

I said, 'We must go now. It is time.'

'And we will come back when it is safe again?'

'Yes,' I lied. 'We will come back.' I moved forward a yard, holding the rifle casually but coveringly. The old man stared. 'You go first,' I urged. 'Say goodbye if you like, but hurry.'

He looked despairingly round the crypt and half turned towards the exit. I thought exultantly, *He's going to go*. Then he stared at me again under the dim light.

He said, 'You are the man that was here before, with the Bland. You are an enemy. He warned me.' He retreated away from the tunnel, into the corner by the record player. The Berlioz was nearing the end of the Oraison. He darted a suspicious look at the case of explosive canted up on the primacord drum. 'You want to destroy my saints. Why?'

'You should hardly need to ask that.'

'You are English?'

'Yes.'

'Then they are your saints. For all of us in Europe they are the saints who will rise again to lead us against the hordes. They do not belong to Germany. Perhaps they do not even belong to Europe — Bland can see no further than Europe. They belong to the human race.'

'The *white* human race.'

'The others are the hordes.' He was shuffling forward, on his knee now. 'Leave this place,' he implored. 'Destroy the mine if you wish, but leave this place whole, and us in it. I will stay. You must leave the little hope for the world. Even hope buried in a mountain side, so that one day the world can find it again. I will stay.'

If I could have held the bayonet at his throat it might have made him move. But his head was sunk into the collar of his greatcoat; there wasn't any throat to be seen. He started to cry. His narrow shoulders shook and a scratchy sob burst from his mouth. 'If you knew the work I'd done. I had only bones and ashes and charred organs…'

'Shut up!' I was feeling sick enough already. I'd got a hand inside the waistband of my slacks and was cautiously feeling the wound. It didn't seem very big but it throbbed like hell. I added more gently, 'Come on out now and we'll let you go. You're no problem. It's Bland who is the danger. You're just an anachronism. It's all over long ago and no one told you. This lot' — I gestured about me — 'is just a lot of junk. The props left over from the epic they made last time. It's old and dead and decaying.'

The music had changed into the Apotheosis, quickening, stirring, proclaiming jubilation instead of grief.

I said, 'And pinching Berlioz is the last straw.'

'Berlioz is of Europe.'

'Not your Europe. Mine.'

He said, 'I stay here.'

'I won't let you. It is all to be blown up.'

'I will still stay.'

'I couldn't let you. You see, I've got to do the blowing up.'

I leaned over and took the cloth of his shoulder and tried to pull him. It felt damp and mossy, like clothes that have hung in the garage for years. Then he twisted away. What happened next is still fuzzy. It happened so fast and so furtively. He was rustling in a pocket again. I thought it might be a pistol and instinctively swung the rifle to hit him. But it was something small he'd found, something that he crammed into his mouth.

For a long moment we stared at each other. He was blinking in surprise at himself and perhaps fear, too.

'What did you want to do that for?' I said, for the second time. 'Christ, what did you want to do that for?'

Possibly he had kept the stuff ever since the time they had all carried it and some had used it. For a minute — no, could it have been a minute? — nothing happened. I thought, it's all right, it's lost its potency.

But it hadn't. It had done the worst thing possible and *half* lost it. The old man started to groan. Then he went forward on his knees again and began to rock. A long strangulated retching gripped him and saliva drooled phosphorescently from his mouth, then a denture plate, falling bright pink on to the dark floor. Suddenly his back arched and he fell back, staring up with eyes that already seemed locked. The retching gave way to a terrible gasping and his limbs began to thrash and drum the ground. I fumbled with the bolt of the rifle in the vague hope that it might be loaded. But the bolt was rusted stiff.

A flailing hand caught the needle of the record player. There was a screech and all at once the music was welling out again at full volume, filling the little chamber with triumphant brass and drums and even drowning the old man's agony. I dropped the rifle and dived into the escape tunnel. To this day I cannot remember how I went through it or how long it took or how little. But later I found both knees were skinned raw.

Out of the rat-hole, under the twelfth light again, I scrabbled for the free end of the safety fuse. I had to light a cigarette now and my fingers were suddenly all strangers to each other. Players No. 6 spilled on to the floor, and, with a tinkle, the spare detonator. Must be careful not to tread on it. The music came funnelling down the low shaft, muted but still clear. It had reached the final, exultant choral passage. The voices sounded like real people, little people marching on me with flags and banners.

I got a cigarette going and blew on the end until it was fiery red and pressed it against the fuse. Nothing happened. I remembered I should have cut the end on the slant to expose more of the gunpowder core. Cigarette back in mouth, smoke in eyes. Knife out, blade open. Hack, hack away, a long oblique cross-section. Cigarette again. This time a fizz, a spurt of smoke and sparks. Then I was running, running, running, up the long tunnel with the voices and the brass and the drums throbbing and dying in my ears.

Rogerson had got in about half-way to meet me. As he saw me coming he turned and we ran together. I was too desperate and too breathless to say anything, not that there was much need to say anything. Rogerson said afterwards that one look at my face was enough.

In the seeming brightness of the winding house I stumbled and fell and was up again and stumbling again, gasping and honking like an exhausted pig. Then I felt myself being swung aloft and next minute I was over Rogerson's shoulder and he was jogging down the track towards the fjord. Fifty yards down he swung me off again and I lay in the snow and mud gulping great breaths of air which cauterized the back of my throat.

Rogerson crouched beside me. He was panting, too, but not so desperately. He'd got his hairy raincoat on again. I thought, I'll catch cold. I've left mine down the mine. Then to my surprise I found it in my hand. I must have picked it up even in the moment of flight. I was just starting to wonder if something had gone wrong with the charge when the ground beneath me shuddered — you always feel a big blow before you hear it — and then there was a bang much louder and sharper than I'd expected, and a long rumble that got mixed up with its own echoes that went reverberating round the fjord and with the fluttering and shrieking of the seabirds that scattered into the air.

The winding house rattled audibly and thick white smoke and dust eddied from it, and continued to pour away as the birds wheeled round and conferred and slowly began to circle down to earth again.

CHAPTER FORTY-EIGHT

On the run back to Ny Alesund, Odd sighted something floating in the water and went over to investigate. It was a square of wood that could have been the engine-hatch cover of a motorboat. It was painted light blue. A little further on was an empty life-jacket.

Eight days later the body of Randers was washed ashore on the north side of the fjord, though it was another week before I heard in London. The hands and face were badly burned and there was a gunshot wound in the abdomen. Bland's body was never found, so far as I know. What happened aboard the light blue motorboat in the thin mist that day will have to remain one more mystery. But sometimes I can't sleep at nights for wishing I had been nicer to Randers. He was weak. He was pliant and pleasant and he wanted everyone to like each other, to believe the best in everyone. When he had to assume the worst I think he found amazing strength. It must have been on the journey back to the mine, after the champagne ceremony. All alone, out in the fjord, the far shore just showing through the drizzle — how would you choose the moment, how would you nerve yourself for action? I wouldn't know.

The Governor's boat carried us back to Longyear. In the hospital there the doctor put one stitch into my bayonet wound. It wasn't much. Gregg had been admitted for his leg to be reset. I saw him for a minute. Aboard the *Bellsund* again there were some curious looks, but Rogerson was well known to the officers. He told them some story. In time, I believe, rumours got around. At this stage no one seemed to suspect anything.

Rogerson shared my cabin now. But as the staggering and awful thing we had encountered stopped dinning in our ears we began to find out we didn't have much else in common.

'What a pity,' he said over a moody drink the second day out of Longyear, 'that such a good idea — the camp, I mean — had to be tainted like that.'

I said, 'Can't you see that it was the camp that was the menace? The stuff in the mine was only the trimmings. Bland may never have intended to use it. Christ, he didn't need to! He had that little Finnish girl eating out of his hand on the name Spartapol alone. There's a tremendous hunger when you're young, a hunger for — for *Romance*. You know, in the sense of the Romantic Revival. And it's only the wicked bastards who can ever cater for it.'

We also had news of Dancer at last. 'He's back home in Brighton,' said Rogerson brusquely, 'minus two front teeth and the money he was carrying. He went ashore, drank too much schnapps, and tried to pick up a sailor. The sailor didn't like it. It was hard to trace him because he gave a false name at first, and said he was an American. You didn't tell me he was one of those.'

'I didn't know,' I said wearily. 'I take people as they come. Haven't you noticed?'

Inevitably I saw less of the girls. Then on the last evening the sun shone royally as the ship slipped past chains of skerries and green islets and there was dancing on deck to an accordion. I danced with Ilse. She was lighter on her feet than she looked; her hair was wiry against my cheek. I danced with Maia. She had the white fluffy jumper on again; she didn't look up. We danced until past midnight, when the sun was low and golden.

Next day I saw them both for the last time. They were staying at the youth hostel in Tromsø for a night before catching the bus to Finland. We met by chance in the dusty main street. They had teamed up with a pair of boys, a couple of the young mid-century *wandervogeln* you find in any youth hostel in Europe, from the Arctic to the South of Spain. They were big and tanned, with hard brown legs and check shirts open to the waist. But they wore sandals and were growing beards, and one carried a guitar and both had eyes that were still vulnerable.

We stood awkwardly in the street and exchanged addresses.

At least, Ilse wrote down, mine and I wrote down theirs. The two vagabonds looked on tolerantly; already the community of dormitories and shared food and cold-water ablutions enclosed them with the girls in an intimacy which a non-hosteller could never penetrate. Maia was smiling almost warmly. Perhaps she felt it too. She was wearing a little brooch. I looked. It must have been the one that Peter had given her. It said *Eton* & *Slough Young Conservatives*.

The seaplane station at Tromsø was a wooden hut by the water's edge a mile or two from town. The dusty double windows crawled with tiny moths and bugs and winged things the colour of old dried grass. There were fly-stained posters on the walls, one advertising Japan, of all places. The passengers for the midnight Ju-plane sat, stood and leaned and waited. It was one of those places where life comes to a point of rest.

I'd left Rogerson at the hotel. He had to clear up some of the aftermath of the affair and Tromsø, as the administrative centre for Spitsbergen, was as good a place as any. Rogerson, Peter, Ilse, Maia, Gregg — I probably wouldn't see any of them again. Randers was the only one who had overlapped my life in London, my separate life, my *real-life* life.

Maia: she was really a very silly little girl. At first the attraction had been nostalgic; I'd tried to recapture the sort of crush you get at fourteen. After that she'd become a symbol, a prize. Would Bland's kind of corruption win her, or mine? Bland had been winning easily. But Ilse: Ilse had been my victory. I felt a love for her, and wanted her; the last night on the boat I'd longed for her until I ached. If only her acquiescence were not like the bars of a cage! If only her toes weren't crooked. I felt in my pocket. I had the slip of paper with her address. Perhaps next year…

In the waiting shed there was a movement towards the door. I picked up my bag and hurried to get out with the leaders and down the long wooden jetty to the waiting seaplane.

A NOTE TO THE READER

If you have enjoyed this novel enough to leave a review on **Amazon** and **Goodreads**, then we would be truly grateful.

Sapere Books

Sapere Books is an exciting new publisher of brilliant fiction and popular history.

To find out more about our latest releases and our monthly bargain books visit our website:
saperebooks.com

Printed in Great Britain
by Amazon

46468364R00155